Quantitative Data Analysis

Willem Mertens • Amedeo Pugliese •
Jan Recker

Quantitative Data Analysis

A Companion for Accounting and Information Systems Research

 Springer

Willem Mertens
QUT Business School
Queensland University of Technology
Brisbane, Queensland
Australia

Amedeo Pugliese
Dept. of Economics and Management
University of Padova
Padova, Italy

School of Accountancy
Queensland University of Technology
Brisbane, Queensland
Australia

Jan Recker
QUT Business School
Queensland University of Technology
Brisbane, Queensland
Australia

ISBN 978-3-319-82640-0   ISBN 978-3-319-42700-3   (eBook)
DOI 10.1007/978-3-319-42700-3

Printed on acid-free paper

This Springer imprint is published by Springer Nature
The registered company is Springer International Publishing AG Switzerland

Preface

Quantitative Data Analysis for Accounting and Information Systems Research guides postgraduate research students and early career researchers in choosing and executing appropriate data analysis methods to answer their research questions. It supports researchers when they are planning to collect data and when they have data that they want to analyze. Using a variety of examples and lay language, this book provides hands-on guidelines on (1) when to use which data analysis method, (2) what kind of data and data structure are required for each of the methods, (3) what each method does and how the methods should be used, and (4) how to report results.

This book is not intended to provide an exhaustive overview of data-analysis methods, nor does it explain the methods in depth. Instead, it guides researchers in applying the right methods in the right way. More skilled researchers can also use the book to refresh their knowledge or as a checklist to avoid skipping important steps. It explains the most commonly used methods in an intuitive and hands-on way, pointing out more advanced resources along the way. As such, it does not aspire to compete with manuals like those of Stevens [1], Field [2], or Crawley [3]. We are not statisticians but researchers who apply statistics,[1] so the book covers the issues that commonly affect others like us, who are engaging in quantitative empirical research.

Quantitative Data Analysis for Accounting and Information Systems Research is the book we would have liked to have had as a support in our own research. Every chapter provides an unintimidating starting point for building your data-analysis skills, the information required to run the most common analyses and report them, and pointers to more extensive resources. At the risk of saying things that may not be *entirely* true in the purest statistical sense, we try to keep the language of this book as simple as possible. As such, the book is brief and written in a language that we hope everyone can understand—from students to researchers to people who wish to study the organizations in which they work. Our goal is to help you conduct academic research of high quality and do the right things right—not to make you a

---

[1] If you are a statistician or simply more observant than we are, we invite you to tell us if you identify an error.

statistics expert—so this book is not about statistics but about *applying statistics* to the research questions that keep you awake at night. (We doubt these questions are about collinearity, but if they are, this may not be the book you are looking for.)

In brief, this book is a software-independent starting point for answering the question: What methods do I use to answer my research questions and how?

We hope you have fun!

Brisbane, QLD, Australia   Willem Mertens
Padova, Italy   Amedeo Pugliese
                                                                                       Jan Recker

References

1. Stevens JP (2009) Applied multivariate statistics for the social sciences. Taylor and Francis, LLC, London
2. Field AP (2013) Discovering statistics using IBM SPSS statistics, and sex and drugs and rock 'n' roll, 4th edn. Sage, London
3. Crawley MJ (2013) The R book, 2nd edn. Wiley, West Sussex

Acknowledgments

Many people have contributed to the development of this book and its content. We are grateful to everyone who helped us discover, explain, and write down our understanding of what matters in using statistics for data analysis. Although there are many of you out there, we would like to thank a few in particular.

First, we are grateful for the support of the QUT's School of Management, School of Accountancy and Information Systems School, for supporting us in the development and conduct of the Advanced Data Analysis workshop series; this book would not have been possible without it. Special thanks go to Professor Michael Rosemann and Professor Peter Green for their inspiring entrepreneurial spirit, flexibility, and support. Second, we are grateful that so many of our colleagues and students attended these workshops and discussed and challenged our understanding of data analysis methods and the way we taught them.

Finally, the ones that contributed—or perhaps suffered—most are our lovely wives, Laura, Claudia, and Laura. Thank you for your support, your patience, and for sharing some of our headaches. You make our lives 89% more enjoyable ($p < .001$, [75–100]).

September 2016

Willem Mertens
Amedeo Pugliese
Jan Recker

Contents

Introduction

Data, data, data. More data is available to us now than ever before. As work and private activities are increasingly facilitated and enacted by our digital devices, we leave traces that can be picked up and analyzed anytime and anywhere. Data collected through surveys, archives, and experiments also remain relevant, as digital traces do not necessarily reflect perceptions, attitudes, and intentions. What also has not changed is that data is meaningless until it is analyzed. That is what this book is about: analyzing data. More precisely: analyzing quantitative data. Numbers.

Data analysis is an iterative process of manipulating and interpreting numbers to extract meaning from them—answer research questions, test hypotheses, or explore meanings that can be derived inductively from the data. This exploration is the first step of any data analysis: we run a few basic manipulations and tests to summarize the data in meaningful statistics, such as means and standard deviations; we visualize the data; and we try to improve our understanding of the information in the data.

Of course, before you can start analyzing, you need to obtain data and have a rough idea of the meaning you want to extract through analysis. Therefore, every chapter briefly discusses *when and why* you may want to use the methods discussed in that chapter, including the type of questions typically answered and the type of data analyzed using that method. We hope that this approach will help you understand how theory, research designs, research questions, data, and analysis depend on one another. The credibility of data is derived from the research design; and the credibility of data analysis is derived from its grounding in theory.

Before we start discussing data analysis methods, we want to summarize the key concepts used in this book and give you a roadmap for using the book and choosing the right analysis method.

© Springer International Publishing Switzerland 2017
W. Mertens et al., *Quantitative Data Analysis*, DOI 10.1007/978-3-319-42700-3_1

1.1   Introduction to the Basics

Before we dive into the wonderful world of applied empirical research and quantitative data analysis, there are a few basic words and rules we will summarize quickly. Everyone reading this book may already have this knowledge, but it never hurts to make sure we speak the same language.

Let's start with the very basics:

A *case* is a person, team, organization, IT system, or any subject or object that is the primary unit of analysis. What constitutes a case is not given but an important decision that we discuss in detail in Chap. 8 of this book, when we talk about structuring data. Many other terms can be used to refer to a case, such as a *unit*, a *subject*, a *respondent,* or any relevant unit of analysis (e.g., store, board member).

A *variable* is an attribute of a case that can change into any one of a set of values. It is called a variable because the values change—the meaning of the variable varies (hence the name). One of the variables related to humans is age because our age changes throughout our lives and because one human's age is not the same as another's. That makes age different from, say, the speed of light, which Einstein showed us to be a *constant*—it never changes.

There are several types of variables: *Categorical* variables do not make assumptions about the distance between the values that the variable may assume, so the values can be <u>nominal</u> (e.g., someone's role as "librarian" or "scientist"), <u>dichotomous</u> (the choice between two values, e.g., gender), or <u>ordinal</u> (e.g., a ranking of intelligence, from normal to literate to smart). *Continuous* variables can take on any value, although there is a difference between truly continuous variables (like time and speed) and discrete variables that jump between whole values without decimals (such as age when measured in years). This difference is important because many sciences (especially the social sciences) measure responses on a quasi-continuous scale, such as a 5-point Likert-type response scale in which the respondent chooses among, for example, "strongly disagree," "disagree," "neutral," "agree," and "strongly agree." These sciences treat such choices as continuous variables, and we do the same in this book.

Most research in social sciences is conducted based on *samples,* not the whole *population.* A sample is that part of a population that is subjected to *observation* (i.e., measurement), which we analyze to draw *inferences* (i.e., draw conclusions based on observation) about the population. For example, if we want to say something about the IT-savviness of Baby Boomers (the population), we could find a *representative* sample of, say, 250 60-year-olds, let them fill out a survey or complete a number of tasks using digital devices while measuring their efficiency and effectiveness, and use the data collected from that particular sample to draw conclusions about Baby Boomers in general. We often call the analysis tools we use to that end *inferential statistics,* because our aim is to infer (i.e., conclude) something about the population from the sample data we have. A *representative* sample means that the characteristics of the sample reflect the characteristics of the larger population. For example, a representative sample of Baby Boomers would not be made up only of men, carpenters, or gadget freaks.

Data refers to any set of values that measure a variable or the combination of all variables for all cases in your study. Sometimes data is collected at several *levels*. For example, we may measure certain attributes of individuals (level 1) or certain attributes of the organizational department to which these individuals belong (level 2). Alternatively, we may measure the same attributes at several points in time. Both scenarios lead to data that is *nested*—that is, the nested variables can have multiple values for a single value of the variables within which they are nested. (Hmmm. . .that was clear as mud, wasn't it?) For example, multiple individuals are nested within one department, so the variable "staff number" is be nested within "department," and one department will have multiple values for "staff number." Got it?

Data collected from cases that are part of your sample are used to test *hypotheses*, which are theoretical statements or predictions that you make about relationships between variables that you expect to occur in the population. For example, a hypothesis about the relationship between the variables "tech savviness" and "age" might be that tech savviness decreases as age increases.

Test statistics help you determine whether the hypotheses are valid by assessing the observed relationships between variables in your sample in light of estimated *summary statistics*, such as means and standard deviations. *Means* are the expected values of the variables, while *standard deviations* are the average distance between the other values you find and that mean. The p-value that is reported as part of the test statistics usually refers to the probability that a test statistic's value would be as high or low if it were only chance that was at play. To conclude the *significance* of an effect we compare the p-value to a predefined *alpha value*, which is the point at which p is considered too small to be determined only by chance (usually 0.05 or 0.01). However, p-values and their corresponding statistics are meaningless without context, as they are but one of many elements that make results relevant and credible. Therefore, they should be reported only along with extensive information about data distributions, effect sizes and the approaches that were used to collect and analyze the data.

One of the many reasons that such is the case is that relying solely on p-values exposes us to the risk of making Type I and Type II errors. A Type I error occurs when you conclude that there is a significant effect when there is none (e.g., a doctor finds that a male patient is pregnant); a Type II error occurs when you find no result when there is one (e.g., a doctor finds that a woman in labor is not pregnant).

If that high-level review leaves you baffled, don't give up! We will go into more detail about each of these terms in the following chapters.

1.2 Navigating the World of Statistics—And This Book

This book is largely about finding the right method for your data and research questions. Figure 1.1 presents a decision framework that is all you will require to achieve just that. So why do you need to read the rest of the book? Proper use of the framework requires a basic knowledge of its components. That is why

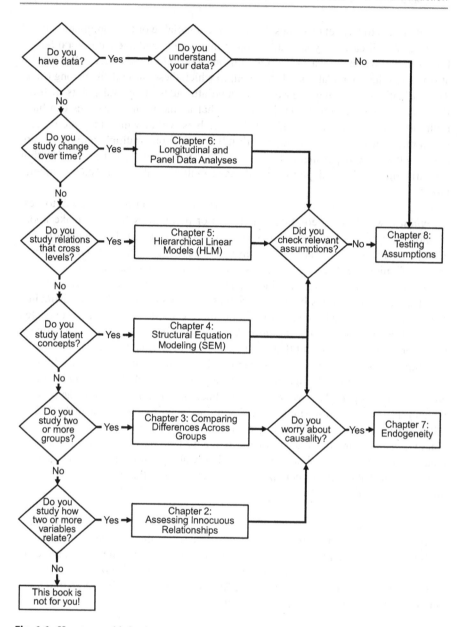

Fig. 1.1 How to use this book

we recommend using this book in an iterative way: use the decision tree to find the method that seems appropriate, read about it, and then reassess your choice. We hope that one such iteration will be enough to solve your most pressing questions, but experience tells us that it will not.

Our recommendation to use the decision tree to determine which chapters to read means that each of the chapters is written so it can be read independently of the others. However, keep in mind that the chapters become increasingly complex, reflecting the increasing complexity of the methods discussed throughout the book.

As Figure 1.1 shows, some of the fundamental challenges in quantitative data analysis are discussed only toward the end of this book: *Can I prove causality? What exactly is contained in my data? What assumptions do I need to be aware of? How do I deal with the ongoing discussion on the use of p-values?* These topics can be complex and tedious, so if you are very new to statistics, we recommend that you browse through the book from start to finish (or answer "no" to every question you do not understand). If you follow this approach and make it to the last chapter of the book, we will reward you with some practical hints and tips on keeping track of your analyses and keeping your mental health as you struggle with mastering complex statistics. Based on how complex your questions and data are, the decision tree takes you backward, step by step, from fairly complex analyses (evaluations involving time, panels, levels, and latent concepts) to fairly simple analyses (differences between groups and relationships between variables).

1.3 What This Book Does Not Cover

We should probably warn you about all the wonderful things you will not find in this book. We start by reiterating that this is not a book about statistics; it's a book about *using* statistics. We use few equations and then only when we think they can help you understand a method. This is not a manual either: for example, we do not provide step-by-step recipes for the perfect regression using SPSS. Although we provide guidance on how to apply methods, we will refer you to other resources for more detailed help.

The book will also not help you design the perfect quantitative study or data collection procedure. Although we provide some advice on both research design and data collection, this advice is inspired by and structured around analysis. More extensive, start-to-end advice on those topics can be found in Recker [4].

Another thing this book does not provide is an exhaustive overview of methods, as we discuss only a selection of methods that are popular in the Accounting and Information Systems research fields. Some analyses, such as discriminant analyses, are too fancy for us to cover, while others, like Bayesian updating, are not very popular in our fields. We also rely heavily on parametric and linear analyses and steer mostly clear of non-parametric and nonlinear analyses.

Finally, in most of what we discuss we concentrate on simple and straightforward scenarios without discussing every little option, variant, or exception. Once you understand the basis of a method, variants and exceptions will not be much of a challenge.

And now on to the rest of the book!

References

1. Crawley MJ (2013) The R book, 2nd edn. Wiley, West Sussex
2. Field AP (2013) Discovering statistics using IBM SPSS statistics: and sex and drugs and rock 'n' roll, 4th edn. Sage, London
3. Stevens JP (2009) Applied multivariate statistics for the social sciences. Taylor and Francis Group, LLC, London
4. Recker J (2012) Scientific research in information systems: A beginner's guide. Springer, Heidelberg

Comparing Differences Across Groups

2

Imagine you want to find out whether people who read statistics books are better at analyzing data than those who do not. You could study this question in at least three ways: (1) You set up an experiment with two groups, one of which you make read a statistics book (a real cruelty), and then you make both groups analyze the same data. (2) You run an experiment with one group only, test their analysis skills, make them read a statistics book, and then test their skills again. (3) You find some people who read statistics books and other people who do not and compare their analysis skills by, for example, studying the number of their quantitative research publications or their grades in statistics classes. All three ways would end up with one variable that tells you whether a person reads statistics books or not—a dichotomous variable that defines group membership—and one continuous variable that summarizes people's analysis skills (or statistics performance). Answering your research question would require you to evaluate whether the analysis skills of the group that read the book are better than those of the other group. This form of group comparisons—comparing one variable score between two groups—is the simplest. This chapter starts from this simple example and adds complexity by adding more groups and variables of interest.

2.1 One or Two Groups

The research question concerning *whether people who read statistics books are better at analyzing data than those who do not*, which requires comparing two groups, is typically answered by using a *t*-test. A *t*-test takes the average score of one group as a reference point and determines whether a second group's average score *differs* from that of the first one by estimating the distance between the two means and comparing that distance to the variance in the data. *Variance*, a measure of how spread out data points are, is calculated by summing up the squared difference between the mean and every raw score (i.e., my skills minus the average, your skills minus the average, then multiplying each of these differences by itself,

© Springer International Publishing Switzerland 2017
W. Mertens et al., *Quantitative Data Analysis*, DOI 10.1007/978-3-319-42700-3_2

which helps to get rid of "negative distances" when the score is smaller than the mean. This process results in one measure of the average squared distance of data points to the mean). A *t*-test calculates the difference between two group means and compares it to the average distance of all data points to the mean.[1]

There are three kinds of *t*-tests, each fitting a certain research design. The first kind is the *independent-samples* *t*-test, which you would use for the first (1) and third (3) study outlined in the first paragraph of this chapter. The independent-samples *t*-test compares the average scores of two **independent samples**, that is, samples whose scores were derived from separate groups of people who were not influenced by each other.[2]

A different situation exists in option (2), so it uses a second kind of *t*-test, the *paired-samples* *t*-test. In the option (2) scenario, there is only one group, but the group's skills are tested twice, once before and once after reading a statistics book. These two scores are **not independent**, as the later score depends to some extent on the earlier score; both scores are for the same group at different points in time.

The third kind of *t*-test is the *one-sample* *t*-test. Although it still compares two means, is does so based on data from one sample only. Imagine, for example, that we are interested in the effect of one particular statistics book only, and that this book has not been published yet. Imagine also that there is one widely accepted test to measure analysis skills for which an overall average (a population average) is available.[3] In this case, we would let one group of people read the book, test their skills using the standard skills test, and compare their average score with the publicly available average score of all other people who have taken the skills test. We are still comparing two groups, but we collect data from only one sample.

How to Analyze and Report Simple Group Comparisons

Imagine we collected the data shown in Table 2.1. A good first step is always to calculate some descriptive statistics. Say that these descriptive statistics tell us that the mean score of people who read statistics is higher ($M_1 = 67.25$) than that of people who do not ($M_2 = 55.75$) and that the standard deviation (the square root of the variance) for both groups is similar at first look ($SD_1 = 19.47$; $SD_2 = 18.51$).

As is the case with most of the tests discussed in this book, the significance of the difference between group averages depends in part on the variance within both groups. If these variances are large, a small difference between the two groups is likely to be insignificant (in other words, it would not be unexpected to find a larger difference). However, if the variances are small (meaning that the individuals in the group have similar analytical skills), even a small difference in the average

---

[1]In fact, depending on the kind of *t*-test, the difference between the means is usually compared only to the variance in *part* of the collected data.

[2]For more information on independence of samples, please refer to Sect. 8.2.

[3]A well-known example of a group of tests for which such reference scores are available is IQ tests. Most common IQ tests have a population average of about 100, so it is easy to evaluate individuals' or groups' scores against that average. A *one-sample* *t*-test would allow you to compare a group average against the population average score of 100.

Person ID	Read stats books?	Analytic skills
1	No	32
2	Yes	61
3	Yes	93
4	Yes	62
5	No	65
6	No	62
7	No	73
8	Yes	87
9	Yes	39
10	No	86
11	Yes	81
...	...	...

Table 2.1 Analytic skills test scores—example

analytical skills between the two groups—one that does and one that does not read statistics books—could be considered significant.

Because variance plays such an important role, you have to test whether the variances in the two groups are close enough to consider the two sets of data homogenous. Homogeneity of variances is one of three *assumptions* that must be checked. (See Sect. 8.2 to learn what assumptions are and how to check them.) In normal circumstances, only the variance of one group is taken into account when calculating the differences between groups. However, if the homogeneity of variances is violated, the one group is not a good representation of the variance in all of the data. In that case, we would have to specify that the variances are not homogenous when calculating the t-test so both variances are taken into account.

The third assumption, alongside independence of samples and equality of variances, is that scores are normally distributed. The t-test is pretty robust against minor violations of this last assumption, but as always it is best to check.

Once these assumptions have been checked, it is time to specify your hypotheses. The null hypothesis (H_0) specifies the reference point—the absence of an effect, while the alternative hypothesis (H_1) postulates that there is a difference between means.

H_0: *The analytic skills of people who read statistics books are equal to those of people who do not read statistics books.*
H_1: *The analytic skills of people who read statistics books are superior to those of people who do not read statistics books.*

The alternative hypothesis (H_1) shown here is an example of a hypothesis that should be tested with a *one-sided* t-test, as we are interested only in whether there is a positive difference between people who do read statistics books and those who do not. If we did not care whether their skills are better or worse but only in whether there is a difference at all, we could use a *two-sided* t-test.

Most statistical software packages allow t-statistics to be calculated in a few straightforward steps. Typically, you specify whether you are interested in a one-sided or two-sided t-test, the α (the threshold at which p is significant—typically 0.05 or 0.01), the reference group, and the test group, and you run the test. Executing these steps based on our fictional data would tell you that people who read statistics books ($M_{do} = 67.25$) do not have significantly better analytic skills than people who do not ($M_{do\ not} = 55.75$; $t = -1.48$, $p = 0.152$). This example also shows how t-tests are typically reported on: You report descriptive statistics (at least the number of participants, the means, and the standard deviations), specify whether it is a one- or two-sided test, present your hypothesis, and report the value for the t-statistic and the level of p at which it was considered significant. If the value was significant, it is customary to report the *alpha* at which it was significant (e.g. $p < 0.05$), rather than the exact p-value. These guidelines also apply to group comparisons with more than two groups and more than two variables, although a larger number of statistics will be reported in such cases.

2.2 More than Two Groups: One-Way ANOVA

We now know that people who read a statistics book do not have significantly better analytic skills than people who do not, but reading one statistics book may simply not be enough. Would reading multiple books help? To test whether such is the case, we could compare the analytic skills of a group that has never read a statistics book, a group that has read one book, and a group that has read two or more books. A t-test is not sufficient to evaluate the differences in skill among three groups, so we use a one-way ANalysis Of VAriance (ANOVA).

Like t-tests, ANOVA models test differences among groups. A disadvantage is that ANOVA tests are always two-sided, while an advantage is that they allow the differences between more than two groups to be tested. As the name suggests, *one-way ANOVA* models evaluate the differences between groups based on one grouping variable and an analysis of the mean and the variance. In doing so, it relies on the F-statistic, which compares the amount of variance that can be explained by group membership to the amount of variance that cannot be explained by the group. Thus, if the F-statistic is low (indicated by a high p-value), splitting the sample into groups does not help to clarify the data much. In our example, a low F-statistic would mean that every group had comparable or seemingly random means and variances, so reading statistics books is not related to people's analytic skills. Because both the mean and the variance are taken into account, ANOVA is pretty robust against violations of the assumptions of homoscedasticity, independence of observations, and normality of observations within the groups [1]. However, regardless of its robustness, it's always necessary to check (and it's always recommended that one correct) (see Sect. 8.2) for violations of the assumptions that underlie the tests.

Similar to t-tests, the null hypothesis in ANOVA states that there are no differences between groups; rejecting that null hypothesis in our example means

Table 2.2 Analytic skills test scores—example with three groups

Person ID	# of statistics books read	Analytic skills
1	2	76
2	1	83
3	1	56
4	0	51
...	...	...

that the number of statistics books someone reads does affect his or her analytic skills. Note that the causality implied in this result is supported by the experimental design only; if the design does not involve an experiment with random assignment of participants to conditions, ANOVA does not allow conclusions to be drawn about the *direction* of relationships. In that case, we would conclude that the number of statistics books someone reads *is related to* his or her analytical skills, rather than that reading statistics books *causes* better analytical skills. We don't know what causes what.

How to Run and Report on a One-Way ANOVA Table 2.2 shows an excerpt of sample data for our example. We now have three groups of people divided according to the number of statistics books they have read—none, one, or more than one. Running a one-way ANOVA test based on this data is, again, pretty straightforward. The variable that defines group membership—in this case, the number of books read—is included as the "factor" or the independent variable. The dependent variable in our example is the participants' analytic skills. Most statistical packages will return an output that includes some version of within-group and between-group sums of squares, which represent the squared average distances to the relevant mean and are used to calculate the F-statistic. Refer to Field ([2])[4] if you want to know the ins and outs of ANOVA, its sums of squares, and the exact calculation of the F-statistic.

If we had a sample of 101 students, the result of the ANOVA test could be reported as follows: "There was a significant relationship between the number of books students read and their analytic skills [$F(2,98) = 6.05, p < 0.01$]." This result suggests that there is a difference between at least two of the three groups. The 2 and the 98 are the degrees of freedom[5] for the F-test. The first number, the 2, is calculated based on the number of groups (k) that are compared, minus one ($k - 1$); the second number, the 98, is the number of people in the sample (n), minus the number of groups compared ($n - k$). Statistical computer programs will always report these numbers alongside other results. Because the degrees of freedom affect

---

[4]Field [2] is an excellent source of detailed guidelines and probably the most entertaining statistics resource ever written.

[5]Although a discussion of degrees of freedom is outside of the scope of this book, the easiest way to explain degrees of freedom is as the number of pieces of information that are taken into account when estimating a statistic or a (set of) parameter(s). Therefore, degrees of freedom are usually calculated based on the sample size and the number of parameters that are estimated.

the calculation of the F-statistic and whether it is significant, you should always include them when you report results.

The ANOVA test result (the F-statistic) tells you that there is a difference between groups, but it does not tell you where the difference lies, how much it is, or whether any two of the three groups differ more or less from the others. After determining whether there is a difference between groups, researchers typically want to know where that difference lies and how much of the variance in the dependent variable is explained by group membership. Let's look at finding where the difference is first: Some statistical programs, such as SPSS, offer the option of running contrasts that compare any two groups at a time according to a set order. For example, a simple contrast compares each group with the first in pairwise comparisons (so: group 1 with group 2, and then group 1 with group 3). While these contrasts help researchers understand the results, they are not as strong as commonly accepted *post hoc tests*. Post hoc tests—after-the-fact tests—allow results to be explored in more detail without abandoning the assumptions made in the main test. For example, a common post hoc test for ANOVA is Fisher's least significant difference (LSD), which runs a set of t-tests between each of the groups but compares differences in means with the overall standard deviation across all groups. As such, it allows researchers to determine which groups score differently without ignoring the fact that more than two groups are being compared.

The other important element in reporting ANOVA results is an estimation of *how much* of the variance in the dependent variable is explained by the groups, referred to as the **effect size**. The effect size is important because a significant effect doesn't necessarily mean that the effect is relevant. For example, consider a finding that people who read two or more statistics books score 9 percent higher on the analytic skills test than those who read none and that this difference is significant (which is possible when the standard deviations in the groups are really small). Would that small difference really be worth reading two or more statistics books? Many people would say no.

We address the difference between significance and relevance further in Chap. 8, but for now let's go back to our ANOVA results. The most common statistics for relevance are *R squared* and *eta squared* (η^2), both of which represent the part of the variance in the dependent variable (analytic skills) that the independent variable (number of books read) explains. A useful summary of rules of thumb for when effect sizes should be considered meaningful is in Kotrlik and Williams [3].

2.3 More than Two Grouping Variables: Factorial ANOVA

Our example explored whether people who read more statistics books have better analytical skills than those who do not, but we may also be interested in the similar effects of taking statistics courses. Now we have two grouping variables of interest: one that defines how many statistics books people have read, and one that defines whether people have taken statistics courses. We are still interested in one

Table 2.3 Example of a 3 × 2 factorial design

	Number of statistics books read		
	0	1	More than 1
No courses taken	Group 1	Group 2	Group 3
Courses taken	Group 4	Group 5	Group 6

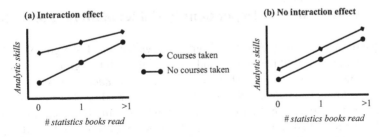

Fig. 2.1   Illustration of an interaction effect in a 3 × 2 design

dependent variable, analytic skills, but two independent variables, statistics books and statistic courses. In other words, we now have a 3 × 2 *factorial design*, which describes a comparison among six groups (Table 2.3).

The approach to running a factorial ANOVA is largely the same as that for a one-way ANOVA, with two additional complexities: two factors have to be included as independent variables and the option to explore an *interaction effect* between these two independent variables. An interaction effect between two independent variables is present when the effect of one independent variable on the dependent variable differs as the other independent variable differs. In our example, an interaction effect would be present if the analytic skills of people who have not taken courses increases more with every extra book they read in comparison to people who have taken courses. Figure 2.1 illustrates an interaction effect, an example of no visible interaction effect, and a main effect for both taking courses and reading statistics books, with both positively related to analytic skills.

To determine whether there is an interaction effect, the ANOVA model must be specified so that the individual effect of each grouping variable (the main effects) and the interaction effect are evaluated. Such specification is achieved by including a third independent variable that is the result of the multiplication of the two independent variables (# of books × courses, no or yes). An F-statistic will be calculated for each variable and for the interaction effect. Again, a p-value lower than the set threshold (e.g. 0.05 or 0.01) means that the variable or interaction has a significant effect on the dependent variable. When the interaction term is significant, it is a good idea to visualize average scores as illustrated in Fig. 2.1.

Results are reported in much the same way as one-way ANOVA results are reported. The only differences are that F-statistics and significance for both variables and the interaction term are reported, and the effect size is reported by using the *partial eta squared* (e.g. *partial $\eta^2 = 0.17$*[6]). As the name suggests, this statistic describes how much of the variance in the dependent variable is explained by one independent term, taking into account that the other independent terms also explain their part.

2.4 More than One Dependent Variable: Multivariate ANOVA

We have discussed examples with one grouping variable and two groups and one grouping variable with three groups, and an example with two grouping variables. What happens if we are interested in more than one *dependent* variable? For example, we may be interested in finding out whether reading statistics books and taking statistics courses not only increase analytical skills but also affect one's attitude toward statistics. In such a case, where we have the same 3×2 design as presented in Table 2.3 (with two dependent variables), we turn to *multivariate ANOVA (MANOVA)*, which can test the effects of each independent variable and their interaction term on the dependent variables, both together and separately. Thus, MANOVA calculates both the *univariate* effects calculated in ANOVA *and* one or more statistics that represent the *multivariate* effect of the independent variables on the dependent variables. The multivariate test statistics take into account that there may be a correlation between the two dependent variables (e.g., if analytic skills are higher, one's attitude toward statistics may be more positive), so independent variables or their interaction term may have a significant multivariate effect on the dependent variables but no univariate effect—or vice versa.

Running and reporting MANOVA analyses is similar to other group comparisons: You describe the groups by summarizing the number of respondents, the mean, and the standard deviation for each group. Table 2.4 provides an example that focuses on means for the groups that result when both grouping variables are combined. An alternative is to show means for both variables separately. Either

Table 2.4 Example of a table with group sizes, means, and standard deviations

		n	Analytic skill M (SD)	Attitude M (SD)
No courses taken	0 books read	18	66.33 (10.35)	2.91 (1.12)
	1 books read	19	69.95 (9.79)	2.73 (1.09)
	more books read	21	71.57 (11.30)	3.01 (0.97)
Courses taken	0 books read	21	69.49 (10.08)	3.54 (1.21)
	1 books read	20	73.59 (12.30)	3.50 (1.13)
	more books read	20	79.51 (9.72)	3.91 (1.06)

---

[6]Depending on the formatting standard that you use, values smaller than 1 will be reported with or without a zero in front of the decimal point. For example, the APA style requires the leading zero only when values can exceed 1.0.

way, make sure to include means, standard deviations, and group sizes so readers can calculate the combinations themselves if they wish.

Next, run the analysis using the two grouping variables as the independent factors, including an interaction term and both dependents. In SPSS, MANCOVA is (accurately) classified as a multivariate General Linear Model. Most statistics programs will return F-statistics and *partial eta squared* values for all univariate effects, and four multivariate statistics: Wilk's lambda, Hotelling's trace, Pillai's trace, and Roy's largest root. Opinion is divided on which of the four multivariate test statistics to report. In a commonly referenced source, Olson [4] expresses a strong preference for the use of Pillai's trace because it usually minimizes the chance of making Type-I errors (i.e., establishing a significant effect when there is none). However, Field [2] adds some nuance to the decision by considering group compositions, sample sizes, and the relative support for assumptions. In most situations, all four multivariate tests statistics will return similar results, so think about why you choose a certain one but don't worry too much about it. As we discuss in Chap. 8, test statistics and their p-values alone do not provide enough information to show meaningful results anyway. Table 2.5 provides an example of how a reporting table might look.

Table 2.5   Example of a MANCOVA reporting table (based on a fictitious sample of $n = 94$)

Effect type	Factor	Statistic	Multivariate effect	Univariate effects Analysis skills	Attitude
Fixed factors	Number of statistics books read	Pillai's trace	0.20		
		$F(4,174) - F(2,87)$[1]	4.63**	7.27**	8.48**
		Partial eta squared	0.10	0.14	0.16
	Whether statistics courses were taken	Pillai's trace	0.01		
		$F(2,86) - F(1,87)$	0.33	0.65	0.42
		Partial eta squared	0.19	0.01	0.01
Covariate	Interest in statistics	Pillai's Trace	0.07		
		$F(2,86) - F(1,87)$	3.34*	0.37	2.12
		Partial eta squared	0.07	0.01	0.02
Interaction effects	Number of statistics books read × statistics courses taken	Pillai's trace	0.08		
		$F(4,174) - F(2,87)$	1.78	1.68	0.89
		Partial eta squared	0.04	0.04	0.02

[a] The first F(df1, df2) refers to the multivariate F-test, and the second refers to the univariate tests of between-subject effects. * $p < 0.05$.; ** $p < 0.01$

2.5   More Advanced Models: Covariance and Repeated Measures

(Multivariate) Analysis of Covariance

All of the models we have discussed thus far assume that only group membership has an effect on the dependent variable, but such is rarely the case. Although research always requires a trade-off between completeness and parsimony (being simple and succinct), there is often at least one variable—a *covariate*[7]—that is not the primary focus of study but that is expected to influence the result dramatically by covarying with group membership and/or the outcome variables. A covariate is a variable that is related to the independent variables, the dependent variables, or both (hence the name—it co-varies). In our example, it is plausible that people with more interest in statistics read more statistics books and take more courses, that they have a more positive attitude toward statistics, and that they have better analytic skills. Even if the whole study were based on a perfectly designed experiment with random assignment to groups, it would be prudent to check for differences in interest in statistics. Doing so calls for the use of Multivariate Analysis of Covariance (MANCOVA).

MANCOVA works in the same way as MANOVA, but it adds a continuous covariance term. It tests whether the grouping variables have an effect on the dependent variables, controlling for potential differences between groups in the covariate. By adding the covariate to the model, all of the variance it explains in the dependent variables will be correctly attributed rather than being confounded with the effect of group membership. You could say that, in our example, adding interest in statistics as a variable avoids erroneously assigning any relationship it has with skills or attitudes to reading statistics books or taking courses. As such, it will likely decrease the effect of our independent variables, but it will rule out the plausible rival theory that results are explained entirely by interest. Ruling out rival theories is an important step in conducting credible research (see Chap. 4 in [5]). Running and reporting a MANCOVA works in the same way as a MANOVA (Table 2.5), although it is often useful to report the statistics for the regression parameters for the covariate as well (e.g., $\beta = 0.01$, $t = 0.23$, $p = 0.82$, partial $\eta^2 = 0.01$).

Analysis of Dependent Groups: Repeated Measures (M)AN(C)OVA

A final variation of group comparisons is used when comparing groups for which the assumption of independence is violated because measures for the dependent variable(s) or covariates are collected from the same participants who have more than one value for the independent grouping variable. For example, we could study the analytic skills of one group of students before, during, and after completion of a statistics course (or after they read zero, one, or all chapters of this book). This case is common in *within-subjects* experimental designs (where our independent

---

[7]A thorough discussion of the role of covariates is presented Chap. 7's discussion of causality, causal claims, and endogeneity issues.

variables measure changes in participants) or in longitudinal studies (where we measure things over time). The primary goal of repeated-measures (M)AN(C)OVA is typically not so much to compare groups of people but to compare how the same people's scores evolve over time.

The advantage of repeated-measures designs is that they usually allow stronger claims of causality. We discuss causality extensively in Chap. 7, but for now let us just say that repeated-measures designs allow the examination of causal relationships because these designs are set up so the cause (reading statistics books) precedes any effect (a change in analytic skills) and because the many confounding factors that are related to the person can be controlled for by including other independent factors or covariates. Controlling for these confounding factors reduces *endogeneity* concerns (which we also discuss in Chap. 7), but the disadvantages of doing so include the possibility of many other factors' confounding the results in the time that passes between two measurement points, and that participants have to take the same test at least twice. These disadvantages may introduce all sorts of problems, including learning effects, fatigue, and drop-out, all of which threaten the reliability of the results. Because the set-up and analysis of longitudinal designs and within-subjects experiments is such a delicate and complex endeavor, we give this topic only a brief look. We discuss other methods for performing longitudinal analysis in Chap. 6, but if repeated-measures (M)AN(C)OVA is what you need, we recommend more specialized resources, such as Stevens [6] and Field [2].

2.6 When to Use Group Comparisons

Regardless of the differences between the various methods of comparing groups, the use of *t*-tests and (M)AN(C)OVA models is generally recommended under the following circumstances:

(a) When you are primarily interested in **exploring differences between groups**, rather than relationships between variables. Although (M)ANCOVA models allow linear relationships between continuous variables to be tested and are classified as one of the general linear models, other members of this class—such as regression and structural equation models—are better suited to assessing linear relationships between variables when group comparisons are not the primary concern.

(b) When exploring differences between groups **based on manifest variables**. Manifest variables are variables that can be directly observed and measured. Latent variables, on the other hand, cannot be directly observed and are measured by means of multiple indicators. These indicators measure the facets of a latent concept and together form the best possible approximation of the concept. One example that we discuss further in Chap. 3 is the ease of use of an IT artifact [7]. Because the ease of use refers to a personal experience, it cannot be readily observed, so users of the artifact are typically asked a range of questions that—together—determine how easy a certain tool is to use. Examples of such questions are *It would be easy for me to become skillful at using this tool*, or *Learning to operate this tool would be easy for me*. These questions are typically rated on a 7-point scale, and scores for the different scales are aggregated to form one score for the latent variable, *ease of use*. Although (M)AN(C)OVA models can be used to run analyses using these aggregated scores, for latent variables, Structural Equation Models (SEM) are recommended instead [8]. We discuss SEM in Chap. 4.

(c) When gathering data through **experiments**. Even when the focus of an experiment is on assessing relationships rather than comparing groups, and even when latent variables are used, (M)AN(C)OVA models are usually the methods of choice for experiments because experiments typically separate treatment groups from control groups. Therefore, we introduce grouping variables (i.e., factors) to represent the experimental conditions.

Once you determine that a group comparison is the most appropriate way to test your hypotheses or analyze your data, you must choose the right group-comparison method, which depends on the number of independent (i.e., grouping) variables and covariates, and the number of dependent variables captured in your design. Table 2.6 summarizes the methods and when each of them should be used.

All of the methods discussed in this chapter are part of the family of General Linear Models (GLM). GLM is an important group of models that also includes the regression models we discuss in Chap. 3. The defining characteristic of GLMs is that they are all based on the assertion that an outcome variable can be predicted by a model that consists of one or more other variables, plus an error. GLM models also assume that this prediction is a linear prediction—that is, the outcome variable changes equally as a result of each equal change in the independent variables in the model—and that the error is normally distributed. (See Chap. 8 to learn more about the normal distribution.) This basic assertion is typically expressed in the form of

Table 2.6 A classification of available group comparisons

	One dependent variable	More than one dependent variable
One group	One-sample *t*-test	Multiple one-sample *t*-tests[a]
Two independent groups	Independent samples *t*-test	MAN(C)OVA
Two dependent groups	Paired-samples *t*-test	Repeated-measures MAN(C)OVA
More than two independent groups	AN(C)OVA	MAN(C)OVA
More than two dependent groups	Repeated-measures AN(C)OVA	Repeated-measures MAN(C)OVA

[a]Considerable discussion surrounds the execution of multiple significance tests on the same data. Typically, it is recommended that a Bonferroni correction be applied, which means dividing α (the threshold at which p is considered significant) by the number of tests performed. Some argue that clearly describing the procedure may be sufficient [9], but we recommend that you both clearly describe your procedure *and* apply corrective measures for multiple tests.

equations, such as Eq. 3.1, which we explain in the first part of Chap. 3. More complex GLMs combine multiple such equations and use the outcome of one equation as a predictor in another (set of) linear equations.

Although this is all very interesting (of course), we warned you that this book is not about statistics, so let us move on to investigating why, when, and how we should turn to regression models.

References

1. Finch H (2005) Comparison of the performance of nonparametric and parametric MANOVA test statistics when assumptions are violated. Methodology 1:27–38. doi:10.1027/1614-1881. 1.1.27
2. Field AP (2013) Discovering statistics using IBM SPSS statistics: and sex and drugs and rock 'n' roll, 4th edn. Sage, London
3. Kotrlik JW, Williams HA (2003) The incorporation of effect size in information technology, learning, and performance research. Inf Technol Learn Perform J 21(1):1–7
4. Olson CL (1979) Practical considerations in choosing a MANOVA test statistic: a rejoinder to Stevens. Psychol Bull 86(6):1350–1352
5. Recker J (2012) Scientific research in information systems: a beginner's guide. Springer, Heidelberg
6. Stevens JP (2009) Applied multivariate statistics for the social sciences. Taylor and Francis, London
7. Davis FD (1989) Perceived usefulness, perceived ease of use, and user acceptance of information technology. MIS Q 13:319–340
8. Cole DA, Maxwell SE, Arvey R, Salas E (1993) Multivariate group comparisons of variable systems: MANOVA and structural equation modeling. Psychol Bull 114(1):174–184
9. Perneger TV (1998) What's wrong with Bonferroni adjustments. BMJ 316:1236–1238

Assessing (Innocuous) Relationships

3

Have you ever submitted a research paper to an academic conference and had reviews come back? If so, you know that conference papers are scored on a range of criteria, including originality, clarity, significance, and methodology. Have you ever wondered which of these criteria really affects whether a paper is accepted or rejected for presentation at the conference?

To answer this question, we examine the relationship between one or more variables on the input side (in this case, originality, clarity, significance, methodology, and any other review criteria) and a variable on the output side (in this case, the acceptance/non-acceptance decision). This example is a case for a regression model, that is, an analysis to assess the extent of a *relationship between several independent variables and a dependent variable*. The difference from the group comparisons in Chap. 2 is that we don't look at how two or more groups differ from each other based on some variables but at how two or more variables relate to each other, taking into account the possible impact of additional variables, known as "controls."

This chapter introduces the most common forms of regression models as a way to assess seemingly innocuous relationships between variables.

3.1   What Are Regression Models?

Regression models are a class of analysis technique that can reveal information about the relationship between several **independent** or **predictor** variables and a **dependent** or **criterion** variable. The computational problem to be solved in regression analysis is to fit a straight line to a number of points such that:

$$Y_i = \alpha_0 + \beta_1 X_1 + \beta_2 X_2 + \cdots \beta_n X_n + \varepsilon_i \qquad (3.1)$$

In Eq. 3.1, Y is our dependent variable (the acceptance decision about a paper submitted to a conference in our example). The terms x_1, x_2, ..., x_n denote one or

© Springer International Publishing Switzerland 2017
W. Mertens et al., *Quantitative Data Analysis*, DOI 10.1007/978-3-319-42700-3_3

more independent variables (the review criteria). The term α_0 is the point where we start, called the intercept. The terms β_1 to β_n are weights between 0 and 1 assigned to each variable that determine their relevance or importance. e is the "error" that denotes a part of the equation we cannot solve.

Regression analysis techniques or models reveal patterns or relationships in the data by determining how two or more variables relate to each other, the basis of many standard research questions. For example, if you are wondering whether spending more money on marketing will increase sales, you need to relate marketing expenditure, as one variable, to sales revenue, as the other. It can get more complex when, for example, you are wondering whether and how age, mileage, engine size, and fuel consumption relate to the price of a second-hand car. In this case, there are several predictor variables—age, mileage, engine size, and fuel consumption—and one outcome variable, sales price.

Let's have a (drastically simplified) look at how the car sales example relates to our Eq. 3.1: The intercept in this example is the average price for any wreck of a car, which we could say, for example, is $1000. Then, whether the car runs well, its age, mileage, and so on will all influence the price at *variable rates* because every car is different. However, we could assume that every mile subtracted from a set average mileage will add a bit to the price, and that how much is added per mile is the same for all cars. That amount is the meaning of the β coefficient, which will differ for each variable—that is, how much the sales price is impacted by mileage, fuel consumption, and so forth differs. Finally, because cars with exactly the same mileage, fuel economy, and so on often sell for slightly different prices, we need an error term to stand for the difference between cases that we cannot explain using the variables in our model.

When there are pairs of variables, the relationship between them can be determined by plotting them. Figure 3.1 shows two "scatter plots" of hypothetical data, which position the values for two pairs of variables as coordinates in a two-dimensional graph.

The two variables in one of the scatter plots in Fig. 3.1 appear to be more closely related than the pair of variables in the other because the data points are in more of a straight line. However, scatter plots tend to be imprecise and their interpretation depends on the presentation of the axes, so they cannot usually reveal the nature of a relationship for certain. What's more, they are restricted to pairs of variables, while we may have three or more variables to relate.

Regression models allow more precise and robust estimations of relations. They operate using a computational measure called *correlation*, which gauges the strength of the relationship between two variables by measuring how closely the points on a scatter plot lie to a straight line (as shown in Fig. 3.2). The correlation coefficient r, which expresses this measure, falls in the range of -1 to 1. If the points lie exactly on the straight line, and the line has a positive slope, $r = 1$. If the points lie exactly on a straight line with a negative slope, $r = -1$. The distances between the points and the straight line illustrate the meaning of the error term e.

Now that we know that correlations are a measure of how closely points in a scatter plot lie to a straight line, we can explain that regression models are attempts

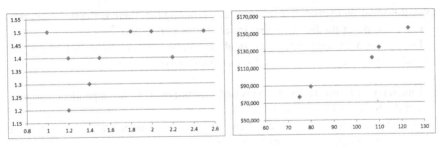

Fig. 3.1 Two scatter plots showing, on the *left*, two pairs of percentage returns on ordinary shares of two companies (one on the x-axis, the other on the y-axis) over 9 consecutive months and, on the *right*, IQ score on the x-axis (as some measure of intelligence) and annual salary on the y-axis (in $)

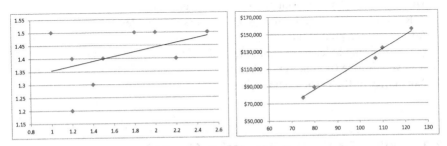

Fig. 3.2 Two scatter plots with *trend lines*. The correlation of the points for the left-hand side is $r = 0.43$, and for the right-hand side $r = 0.99$

to fit a straight line to the data such that we can predict Y from the set of X_s we have (remember Eq. 3.1). You can think of regression models as drawing the perfect straight line into scatter plots such that it is as close as possible to all points in the plot (which is very difficult, if not impossible, to do precisely for data that comes nowhere near a straight line on a scatter plot). Regression models draw this line automatically using an algorithm that *fits* the best straight line to the data.[1] To calculate which straight line best fits the data, regression models use the *coefficient of determination* R^2, which measures the straight line's "goodness of fit" to the data by calculating the proportion of the total sum of squares (i.e., the variance) explained by the straight line. Since the variance is a proportion, it ranges from 0 to 1; you can think of it as a percentage between 0 and 100 %, where a low percentage shows that a straight line really doesn't fit all that well to the data—that is, the regression doesn't work.

The predictive ability of regression models lies in its finding the equation that fits the best straight line; once we have the equation, we can insert values for x_i and

---

[1]The usual way of fitting is by minimizing the *least squares*, that is, the squared distances of error terms between any data point and the line, or the vertical distance between the line and a point, multiplied by itself.

solve the equation to predict Y (always remembering that there is the residual error e, as we can never predict the value for all points perfectly).

Finally, as with any other statistical technique, regression models build on several assumptions (that we will discuss in Chap. 8):

1. **Linearity and additivity** of the relationships between the dependent variable and the independent variables:
    (a) The expected value of dependent variable is a straight-line function of each independent variable, holding the others fixed.
    (b) The slope of that line does not depend on the values of the other variables.
    (c) The effects of different independent variables on the expected value of the dependent variable are additive.
2. **Statistical independence** of the errors
3. **Homoscedasticity** (constant variance) of the errors
    Remember: Variance is equal in different (sub-)samples
    (a) versus the predictions
    (b) versus any independent variable
    (c) versus time (in time series data)
4. **Normality of the error distribution.**

3.2   When Do We Use Regression Models?

We use regression models when we are interested in determining how one or more input variables relate to one dependent variable. In simple terms: you use regression models when you want to:

- predict a dependent variable based on a set of independent variables,
- determine whether a certain independent variable has an effect on a certain dependent variable,
- determine which independent variables "matter" in predicting an independent variable, or
- discriminate among independent variables in terms of how important they are to predicting or explaining a dependent variable.

There are several variants of regression models, and their use depends on the nature of the variables you are interested in. The most common model types are summarized in Table 3.1.

For normal, hierarchical, and logistic regressions (Table 3.1), the following conditions apply:

(a) Independent variables *must be* continuous (e.g., age, weight, salary) or a scale (e.g., a review score from 1 to 10, a measure of agreement from not at all to very much).

Table 3.1 the most common regression models and their core characteristics

Regression model	Main characteristics
"Normal" regression[a]	One or more dependent variables that are continuous/scale variables[b]
	One or more independent variables that are continuous/scale variables
Hierarchical regression	One dependent variable that is a continuous/scale variable
	Multiple blocks with multiple independent variables that are continuous/scale variables
Logistic regression	One dependent variable that is a binary variable
	One or more independent variables that are continuous/scale variables
Other complex regressions[c]	Multiple dependent variables that are continuous/scale variables
	One or more independent variables that are continuous/scale variables

[a]A "normal" regression is also referred to as just "regression" or as "Ordinary Least Squares (OLS) regression"
[b]Single regressions have one dependent variable, and multiple regressions describe cases that have multiple dependent variables
[c]Complex regressions are discussed separately in Chap. 4

(b) There is usually *one dependent variable* to explain or predict, but there could be more, as is the case with variance models (Chap. 2).

(c) The dependent variable is a continuous or scale variable, so it is a *metric* variable.

(d) An exception to point (c) is when the dependent variable is *binary*. In this case, we can run a logistic regression, where the independent factors are evaluated based on their ability to predict whether the dependent variable will be value a or value b (say, male or female).

   With these core features in mind, hierarchical regressions differ in that:

(e) It is possible and purposeful to group the independent variables meaningfully into multiple categories, clusters, groups, or "blocks," where possible means that some variables are semantically related to each other, and purposeful means that such a categorization is relevant to the question or objective of the data analysis.

   In the example of the paper submitted to a conferences, all review criteria belong to the group of review criteria, so they form a meaningful category (i.e., "review criteria"). We could have collected additional data, such as the age of the authors and reviewers and the number of papers the authors and reviewers have submitted. It would have been *possible* to cluster all these variables into the blocks "review criteria," "author criteria," and "reviewer criteria". While it would have been possible to categorize the collected variables, but it wouldn't have been *purposeful* because the research questions asked did not demand a discrimination among or examination of groups of potentially relevant variables.

   Table 3.2 provides a different view on the question concerning when to use which type of statistical model. The table shows how regression models, as one type of model that is appropriate for some data, are related to the family of analysis-of-variance models discussed in Chap. 2 and how they relate to more complex models

Table 3.2 Choice of statistical model for different types of variables

Number and type of *dependent variable*	Number and type of *independent variable*	Preferred statistical model
1	*2 or more*	
Non-metric	Metric	Logistic regression
	Non-metric	Log-linear analysis
Metric	Metric	Linear or hierarchical regression
	Non-metric	Analysis of variance
2 or more	*2 or more*	
Non-metric	Metric	Multivariate multiple regression with dummy variables
	Non-metric	Multivariate analysis of variance with dummy variables
Metric	Metric	Multivariate multiple regression
	Non-metric	Multivariate analysis of variance

that are discussed later in the book. (We do not discuss log-linear analysis in this book at all, but there is good guidance available elsewhere [1].)

3.3   How Do We Examine Regression Models?

As elsewhere in this book, we assume that the researcher has developed a research model with hypotheses and created suitable measurement instruments (e.g., surveys) to measure all variables and collected data that are available. For the purpose of this chapter, we consider the data from the conference paper example in [2]. The data consists of an identifier for the papers submitted for review, a set of six review criteria, an overall rating score for the quality of the paper (which could be considered a seventh review criteria), and the final decision for acceptance or rejection. An excerpt of the data is shown in Table 3.3.

All review criteria were scored on a scale from 1 (lowest score) to 7 (highest score), so these variables are all *metric*, while the "Decision" variable is *binary*– accept or reject. With this data in hand, we can explain how to execute linear regression models (in this section) and logistic regression models (in Sect. 3.5).

Recall that the simplest case of regression models (OLS regressions) has a metric dependent variable and one or more metric independent variables. With the data we have (Table 3.3), we can ask the question: How do the review criteria scores influence the overall evaluation score? In other words, which measure of a paper matters most (or least) to receiving a high rating? Performing a regression analysis to answer this question runs in three steps:

1. **Examine descriptive statistics.**
   As with any other data analysis, we begin by examining descriptive statistics. Since most of our variables are metric, examining the descriptive statistics typically involves reporting means and standard deviations for each variable in

Table 3.3 Excerpt of data used in the conference-paper example [2]

Submission ID	Significance of contribution	Theoretical strength	Methodology used	Presentation	Relevance	Appeal to audience	Overall rating	Decision
173493	5.33	5.67	5.67	6.00	5.67	5.67	5.00	Accept
173781	5.00	5.00	4.67	5.67	5.00	5.33	4.67	Accept
174068	4.00	3.00	4.00	3.33	4.00	3.33	3.00	Reject
174355	4.50	3.75	3.25	5.00	5.50	4.75	3.75	Reject
174642	1.50	2.50	2.00	2.50	2.50	2.50	1.50	Reject
175499	5.00	4.67	4.00	4.67	4.67	4.33	3.67	Accept
⋯	⋯	⋯	⋯	⋯	⋯	⋯	⋯	⋯

order to get *initial insights* into the data, such as which review criterion scored the highest or lowest and the overall level of scores given to papers (i.e., are they viewed positively or negatively on average) For example, "relevance to conference" consistently scored higher than any other review criteria, so the conference paper submissions were generally viewed as being relevant to the conference [2].

A second item we can evaluate through descriptive statistics is whether there is *sufficient variation* in the data. The standard deviations provide such information. If the standard deviation is reasonably high—often using the threshold of more than 1.00—we can assume that the data has a sufficient number of papers (in this example) that were scored high or a sufficient number that were scored low. If the standard deviation is low, most papers were scored consistently and similar to the reported mean, which could lead to problems in the statistical testing because a variety of values in the independent variables is needed to estimate and predict different values of a dependent variable. In other words, if one variable behaved too much like a constant (i.e., all values are identical or close to identical), it would not be a *variable!*

2. **Screen the data for assumptions.**

As with any other data analysis, regression models have a set of assumptions that must be met. Here we focus on one assumption, which is the absence of *multicollinearity*. The presence of multicollinearity indicates that two or more predictor variables in a regression model are highly correlated such that one can be linearly predicted from the others with a substantial degree of accuracy. In regression *we want to have high correlations* (Fig. 3.2) *but not too high!* Correlations that are too high (e.g., higher than 0.80) mean that you can infer one variable from the other, as they are not sufficiently distinct from each other. Multicollinearity does not reduce the predictive power or reliability of the analyses, but it may affect the individual estimates for effect sizes and magnify the standard errors [3]. If that is the case, the statistical metrics (such as the *beta* and *p* coefficients) may not be as reliable as we would like them to be.

We screen for multicollinearity by examining the pairwise correlations between all variables. The rule of thumb is to examine (and report!) correlations between variables and, if some of the predictor (independent) variables are pairwise correlated with a coefficient higher than 0.75, it means that in the analysis that follows we should check for multicollinearity by including additional metrics that would normally not be estimated or reported, particularly the tolerance level and Variance Inflation Factor (VIF) [3].

3. **Estimate the regression model.**

Assuming our assumptions are not violated, we then estimate a regression model, specifying:

(a) our dependent variable—in our example, the variable "Overall rating"
(b) our independent variable(s)—in our example, the six variables Significance of contribution, Theoretical strength, Methodology used, Presentation, Relevance, and Appeal to audience (Table 3.2)

(c) How the regression model estimation should be conducted—given more than one independent variable, build the regressions in one of three ways:

    (i) "Enter"—enter all variables at the same time into the model and run the analysis.

    (ii) "Step-wise forward"—enter variables into the model one at a time, with one variable in the first regression model and additional variables added one at a time until all variables have been added or a variable entered does not significantly improve the model's ability to predict values for the dependent variable.

    (iii) "Step-wise backward"—enter all variables into the initial model and then remove them one at a time when they are irrelevant (i.e., insignificant) predictors of the dependent variables until the model contains only "relevant" variables.

A good rule of thumb is to try all three variants of estimation, typically in the order suggested. It may also make sense to enter different combinations of variables into the model in order to explore the results' sensitivity relative to the variables considered. This suggestion is good practice for all types of quantitative data analyses even though it is not usually seen in papers, most of which report on one analysis after spending countless hours trying different approaches. On the other hand, trying enough combinations will eventually lead to a relationship that is statistically significant but not necessarily *meaningful*. This kind of result is not useful either, so make sure to keep your theory in mind while experimenting with analyses. It is easy to find results in statistics, but the goal of analysis is extracting *meaning*, not finding a coefficient that is above or below some threshold.

Independent from the model estimation, at least two sets of results should be produced: overall model fit and parameter estimates.

Overall model fit is an omnibus (i.e., "everything") test that determines whether the regression model specified as a whole fits the data well—that is, whether the regression model with the specified independent and dependent factors is a good match to the observed correlations (i.e., the actual characteristics of your data). The fit test contains two key measures: the R^2 coefficient and an F statistic based on a comparison between the estimated model and an 'empty' model.

The R^2 coefficient measures the proportion of variance in the dependent variable (in our example, the overall rating) that can be explained by the independent variables (in our example, all six review criteria). R^2 is an overall measure of the strength of association but it does not reflect the extent to which any particular independent variable is associated with the dependent variable. It ranges between 0 and 1, with the optimum score being as close to possible to 1.

Since even a high R^2 value does not mean that the statistical model matches the characteristics of the data very well—you might get a high R^2 value by chance—the omnibus test also compares the regression models against a second regression model in which all coefficients are set to zero. In other words, it compares the predictors we assume affect the dependent variable against a model with no predictors that tries to predict the values of the dependent variable by guessing.

The form of this test should sound familiar from Chap. 2, as it is an ANOVA test between two groups: our regression model against the empty model. Like any other ANOVA test, it examines variance (e.g., the sum of squares), degrees of freedom, and the F statistic. If the F statistic is significant, the regression model is significantly different from an empty model, so it provides a substantially better explanation of the dependent variable than guessing does. If it does not, it's time to look for a better model.

Parameter estimates concern the computation of coefficients for all the variables in our model. Remember Eq. 3.1? Parameter estimates reveal the values of the terms β_1–β_n (between 0 and 1) so we can gauge each variable's importance in predicting the dependent variable.

Estimation of parameters computes several values:

(a) The value of the intercept α_o, also called the constant—The constant is usually not all that interesting to most studies, as it expresses the value of the dependent variable when all predictors are set to 0, a rarity in reality.

(b) Unstandardized and standardized coefficients for our terms b_1–b_n—The unstandardized coefficients B are the values of the terms b_1–b_n in our equation, that is, the values for the regression equation in predicting the dependent variable from the independent variable. However, we are usually interested in the standardized coefficients *Beta*, the coefficients you would obtain if you standardized all of the variables (both dependent and independent) in the regression before estimating the model. Standardization normalizes them so they are all measured on the same scale (say, from 0 to 100) because, in most cases, the variables' values, even though they are all metric, are not measured on the same scale. For example, age is measured on a different scale than IQ or height. By standardizing the variables before running the regression, you put all of the variables on the same scale so they are comparable and you can see which one has a larger effect. In other words, the standardized *Beta* coefficients describe the *importance* of a variable in affecting the value of the dependent variable.

(c) *t*-values and *p*-values (significance levels) for each variable—These are the *t*-statistics and their associated 2-tailed *p*-values that are used to determine whether a variable's coefficient is significantly different from zero. We typically look for variables that have high *t*-statistics and low *p*-values (below the typically recommended threshold of $p < 0.05$). Together, the *t*-statistics and *p*-values describe a variable's *relevance* (although a low *p*-value is not enough; see Chap. 8 for a discussion on the use of *p*-values).

3.4   How Do We Report Regression Analyses?

Reporting on regression models involves four elements:

1. **Descriptive statistics** about the distribution (e.g. means, median, standard deviation, skewness) of all variables—We typically report at least means and standard deviations, but if assumptions are even partially violated (see point 2 below), report statistics like skewness, median, and range.
2. **Testing of assumptions**—This reporting involves explaining the assumptions that are violated (if any) and any measures taken to deal with the violation.
3. **Overall model fit statistics**, particularly the F statistics, including the associated degrees of freedom and the R^2 coefficient.
4. **Parameter estimates** for the independent variables and the constant—At minimum, this reporting includes the standardized *Beta*, the t-value, and significance levels. A good practice involves also reporting the 95 % confidence interval lower and upper bounds for the unstandardized B coefficients (if reported).

Let's have a look at common reporting practices (from [2], pp. 293–294):

> [...] we conducted a stepwise linear regression analysis [3], using the overall evaluation score as the dependent variable and the review criteria as the independent variables. The [...] stepwise regressions [...] showed that all of the review criteria scores were significantly associated with the overall evaluation score. Therefore, all of the review criteria entered the [...] final regression models shown [...].
>
> [...]
> We first examine collinearity statistics. Multicollinearity is present when tolerance is close to 0 (Tolerance < 0.01; see [3]) or the VIF is high (VIF > 10), in which case the *beta* and p coefficients may be unstable. The VIF and tolerance measures [...] suggest that multicollinearity is not an issue in the data for any of our three conferences. The Appendix further shows that the data also meet accepted criteria for the Condition Index (<30) and proportions of variance between two or more variables ($p < 0.50$), both of which also indicate that multicollinearity is not present.

This text excerpt shows how the reporting explains the type of regression model estimation used (stepwise forward regression) and how a particular finding during data screening (i.e., the potential bias stemming from multicollinearity) was incorporated into the analysis and reported. (Recall that multicollinearity may destabilize the parameter estimates.) To determine whether multicollinearity is present because of high correlations among independent variables (above 0.75), we estimate and report additional statistics (e.g., tolerance and VIF), as shown in Table 3.4. A commonly used rule of thumb in interpreting VIFs involves determining whether any of the predictors has an associated VIF that is larger than 3. (Some authors impose less stringent requirements and pose a VIF of 10 or above as a warning threshold.) If VIFs are lower than the threshold, then we can assume that multicollinearity does not plague our results. Even if such a bias were present, reporting all relevant values would allow the reader to interpret the data for himself

Table 3.4 Excerpt of regression analysis results reported in [2]

Review criterion	Adjusted R^2 F (df1, df2)	Beta	p-value	Tolerance	VIF
Significance/contribution	0.83 F (6, 573) = 476.44	0.36	0.00	0.24	4.14
Theoretical strength		0.22	0.00	0.31	3.26
Appeal to audience		0.16	0.00	0.24	4.16
Presentation		0.14	0.00	0.43	2.31
Methodology used		0.11	0.00	0.34	2.93
Relevance to conference		0.06	0.02	0.38	2.63

or herself, gauge the data's conclusiveness and robustness, and determine the resulting implications.

Table 3.3 summarizes all relevant output from the regression model estimation. Table 3.3 gives the relevant statistics for overall model fit, particularly the F statistic (which we can look up in an F distribution table like http://www. danielsoper.com/statcalc3/calc.aspx?id=4 to show that the statistic is significant) and the R^2 coefficient, which is reasonably high. Table 3.3 also shows the relevant values for gauging relevance, viz., the standardized Beta coefficient and the p-value associated with the variable's t-statistic.

Note. In this example we reported the VIFs because the descriptive statistics indicate some concerns about multicollinearity. As the VIFs and the other additional tests show, this concern was unfounded.

3.5   What If...

In the previous sections we assumed the dependent variable was metric and independent could not be meaningfully grouped; what if this is not the case? Then we turn two other variants of regression models: logistic regression and hierarchical regression.

Logistic Regressions

Logistic regression models are linear regressions, except the dependent variable is **binary** instead of *metric*. In our example, a suitable variable is the "Decision," which can take one of two values: accept or reject. To answer the question concerning whether any of the review criteria is relevant (and if so, how important it is) to the acceptance/rejection decision, we run a logistic regression. This question makes good sense because the overall rating, which we can predict reasonably well, does not guarantee a paper's acceptance because, as the conference's submission guidelines state,

"program committee members and track chairs typically rank the papers based on the overall evaluation score and consider the subjective, written reviews, in addition to the objective scores. Written comments support the reviewer's decision and also provide input to the paper's authors as to how the paper might be improved. [...] Other factors such as the number of submissions per track, and so on, may also influence the final acceptance decision." ([2], p. 289)

Logistic regressions estimate the probability of a binary response based on one or more predictor (or independent) variables. Although logistic regressions run analogous to linear regression, logistic regression assumes a different distribution of the dependent variable given the independent variables. Logistic regression estimates the **probabilities** of two outcomes, not the shared variance. There are several forms of logistic regression, but the case we are discussing here is a simple binary logistic regression.

The binary logistic regression converts a binary variable into a continuous variable that can take on any real value (negative or positive) by means of the logit function,[2] which creates a continuous criterion as a transformed version of the dependent variable. Then the logit-transformed dependent variable can fit to the predictors in the same way that a linear regression would. Once we have the parameter estimates, we convert the predicted value of the logit back into predicted odds via the inverse of the natural logarithm (the exponential function).

Knowing the predicted odds then informs how the logistic regression is conducted. When we "fit" the regression model to the data, we evaluate the success of the logit function much in the same way that we evaluate overall model fit for a linear regression: we statistically evaluate whether the logit model based on our predictors is a better fit to the data (using Chi-square as the fit measure) than a model with no predictor. Then we evaluate whether the model is any good at explaining the outcome variable. In linear regression we would use the R^2 coefficient, but in logistic regression we use a coefficient called **Pseudo-R^2**. Logistic regression does not have an equivalent to the R^2 coefficient because there is no shared variance that we can measure, although statisticians have tried to come up with a similar measure. Unfortunately, there is a wide variety of Pseudo-R^2 statistics, which can give contradictory conclusions. Therefore, the best practice is to report on several of them and to interpret any or all of them with great caution.

Finally, the parameter estimates in logit regression differ somewhat from those in linear regression: We examine **estimates** that describe the logit regression coefficients. The standard interpretation of the ordered logit coefficient is that, for a one-unit increase in the predictor, the response variable level is expected to change by its respective regression coefficient in the ordered log-odds scale, while the other variables in the model hold constant. In a way, then, the logit coefficients are similar to the *Beta* coefficients, although the logit coefficients are not normalized to the range $[-1, 1]$. However, because the change they describe is related to the ordered log-odds scale (in other words, they are difficult to interpret), we also report on the exponentiations of the estimate as **Exp(B)**, which calculates the odds ratios of the predictors and is easier to digest. Using the example of the

---

[2]The logit function computes the odds of the two binary outcomes happening for different levels of each independent variable. Then it takes the logarithm of the ratio of those odds (which is continuous but cannot be negative).

conference paper, an odds ratio can be interpreted as "the change in the chance that my paper is accepted (vs. rejected) if *originality* increases by 1." This interpretation differs from standardized regression coefficients in normal regressions, which predict the magnitude of change in the dependent variable (e.g., overall quality rating) if *originality* increases by 1. Another difference between linear regression and logit regression is that, in logit regression, we examine the **Wald-statistic** instead of the *t*-statistic to gauge the relevance of that odds change.

The reporting of logistic regression is fairly simple: You still provide a test of assumptions and the measures for overall fit, but you report several Pseudo-R^2 statistics instead of just one, and in describing parameter estimates you report the *Beta* estimates as well as their exponentiation Exp(B) ([2], p. 295). Should you read [2], you will see that the two review criteria "Methodology used" and "Relevance to conference" that we found significant and important in estimating the overall rating are not significant predictors of the probability of a paper's being accepted!

Logistic regressions, that is, regressions that involve the *logit* function, are often discussed with regressions that involve the *probit* function–probit regressions. Both logit and probit regressions transform a completely linear model to yield a nonlinear relationship in order to fit the predictors to the non-metric dependent variable. The difference between logit and probit lies in how this transformation is computed: The logit model uses the cumulative distribution function of the *logistic distribution* (which looks like an S-shaped curve), while the probit model uses the cumulative distribution function of the *standard normal distribution* (the bell curve). Both functions can take any number and rescale it to fall between 0 and 1, then use that new number as a predicted probability. Therefore, the key difference between logit and probit lies in the underlying theory: what do we expect the distribution of the transformed variable to look like?

Both logit and probit models yield similar results, so preferences often come down to popularity. Probit models can be generalized to account for non-constant error variances, so they are preferred in some advanced contexts, but if advanced applications are not needed, it does not matter which method you choose.

Hierarchical Regressions

Finally, we examine hierarchical regressions as a variant of standard linear regressions. Hierarchical regressions should not be confused with hierarchical linear models, which are used for multilevel data (discussed in Chap. 5). Hierarchical regression models ask whether there are meaningful groupings of independent variables, referred to as blocks. Technically speaking, hierarchical regression models are a type of linear **regression** models in which the observations fall into hierarchical or completely nested levels, as defined by the blocks. The question that hierarchical regression models answer concerns not only whether any set of variables is important and relevant to predicting an outcome variable, but also whether any regression model that builds on another regression model improves it in terms of overall model fit). That is, if there is a hierarchy of blocks of variables. The advantage of hierarchical regression models is that they allow one to discriminate between categories or groups of variables. A good example is given in [4], which measures understanding (a metric dependent variable) and provides a model with variables grouped into three categories: control, cognitive abilities, and learning process.

You could just as easily hypothesize that performance, as a dependent variable, is contingent on three other groups of variables: individual factors (e.g., experience, knowledge, motivation), technological factors (e.g., information quality, usefulness), and organizational factors (e.g., culture, management support). Hierarchical regressions clarify what you gain when you start with one group of variables and then add the next and the next to build a hierarchy of nested regression models as part of a larger model.

Hierarchical regression models work the same way as standard linear regressions, with the defining characteristic that all variables are not entered simultaneously into the model but in blocks, such that model 1 contains all variables from one block (say, individual factors), model 2 contains variables from the block in model 1 plus a new block (say, technological factors), model 3 contains model 2 plus a new block, and so on. The estimation then estimates all of these regression models—model 1 in itself, then model 2 and then model 3. Thus, we obtain values for overall model fit and parameter estimates for each model.

Since models 2 and 3 add upon the previous model (s), we increase the **degrees of freedom** with each new model, as we add more and more variables to the equation that we are estimating. In doing so, we hope that we improve the model fit to the data: we hope that we increase our R^2 coefficient as the measure of shared variance explained. For each model change, we can evaluate whether the increase in R^2 is significant, given that we increased the complexity of the equation (i.e., we increased the degrees of freedom). In simpler terms, we evaluate whether an added explanatory power is worth the effort, given that increasing the explanation requires more variables, and our explanation becomes more complex. Complexity is

Table 3.5 Excerpt of hierarchical regression analysis results

Term	1: Control	2: Cognitive abilities	3: Learning process
PDK-1	0.02	0.13	0.03
PMK	0.10	0.03	−0.07
SE	0.10	0.07	0.08
AA		−0.21	−0.25*
SA		0.46**	0.56***
DM			0.01
SM			−0.34**
DS			0.18
SS			0.29*
F	0.62	2.40*	3.04**
F change	0.62	4.97**	3.45**
R^2 change	0.02	0.11*	0.13*
R^2	0.02	0.13	0.26

Source: [4]
*$p < 0.05$; **$p < 0.01$; ***$p < 0.001$

typically regarded a bad thing because, as Einstein said: "If you cannot explain it simply, you do not understand it well enough."

In evaluating and reporting hierarchical regressions, we perform the same steps as in a linear regression, plus, in addition to the R^2 coefficients and F-statistics for each "block" model, we report on the R^2 change between models (e.g., the R^2 value of model 2 minus the R^2 value of model 1) and use the F statistics of each model (which contain their relevant degrees of freedom) to determine whether these changes are significant. Table 3.5 shows an example of the reporting for a hierarchical regression of a comprehension task score (called Comp-D1) ([4], p. 211).

In [4], each new model adds a new block of variables to the regression equation, and the F statistic and R^2 coefficients change. The "best" model achieves the highest R^2 coefficient and improves on the R^2 coefficient and F-statistic over previous models. In other words, adding new blocks of variables improves a model's fit with the data.

References

1. Howell DC (2009) Statistical methods for psychology, 7th edn. Wadsworth Cengage Learning, Belmont, CA
2. Rosemann M, Recker J, Vessey I (2010) An examination of IS conference reviewing practices. Commun Assoc Inf Syst 26:287–304
3. Tabachnick BG, Fidell LS (2001) Using multivariate statistics, 4th edn. Allyn & Bacon, Boston, MA
4. Recker J, Reijers HA, van de Wouw SG (2014) Process model comprehension: the effects of cognitive abilities, learning style, and strategy. Commun Assoc Inf Syst 34:199–222

Models with Latent Concepts and Multiple Relationships: Structural Equation Modeling

4

One of the best-known models in Information Systems research is the Technology Acceptance Model (TAM), which postulates that users will intend to use a system if they find it useful and easy to use, and that they will find a system useful if they find it is easy to use. This model has been studied over and over again, typically by surveying users (or even non-users) of some system with questions about the degree to which they find the system useful and/or easy to use and whether they intend to use it in the future.

The analysis of data to test the TAM is a good example of how data analyses can become increasingly complex. The theoretical model and the example sound simple, but the analysis is statistically: (1) we have multiple relationships between variables, such as the link between perceived ease of use and intention to use but also perceived usefulness; (2) variables such as usefulness, ease of use, and intention to use are measured with multiple items/questions in a survey, so each variable has multiple data points; and (3) usefulness, ease of use, and other concepts are latent–we cannot measure them directly.

This chapter examines structural equation models, one of the most frequently used ways to model data for latent concepts, and introduces structural equation modeling's main principles and most common variations.

4.1 What Are Structural Equation Models?

Structural equation models (SEMs) are multivariate regression models. Multivariate simply means "multi-equation," while the regression models discussed in Chap. 3 are univariate ("single-equation"). The main differences between SEMs and "simple" regression models are that (1) unlike regressions that typically have one dependent measure or variable, SEMs can have several dependent measures or variables, and (2) the dependent measures themselves can appear as predictors for other dependent variables as intermediaries. Consider the example of the TAM:

© Springer International Publishing Switzerland 2017
W. Mertens et al., *Quantitative Data Analysis*, DOI 10.1007/978-3-319-42700-3_4

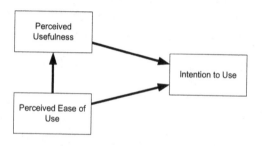

Fig. 4.1 Technology Acceptance Model [1] as a structural model

Figure 4.1 shows the TAM's postulates: Perceived ease of use supposedly influences perceived usefulness—that is, the degree to which users deem a system to be useful—and intention to use—that is, whether users intend to use the system in the future. Perceived usefulness is a dependent (effect) variable for the relationship with Ease of use, as well as an independent (cause) variable for the relationship with Intention to use. In simple regression models, we would have to build three equations in order to depict each of these relationships, but SEMs can run all equations simultaneously (which is why they are often called simultaneous equation models). Running the equations simultaneously provides a significant advantage because we can use the results from one equation (say, how much Ease of use influences Perceived usefulness) directly and simultaneously in estimating the other equations (say, how much Perceived usefulness influences Intention to use).

Another useful feature of SEMs is shown in Fig. 4.2.: SEMs support the use of *measurement items*—sets of multiple data points used to estimate the variables in the model. Often, each measurement item corresponds to a single survey question, and unlike a normal regression there is usually more than one measurement item for each variable in the model.

Imagine we have done what most researchers do and used a survey instrument to gather data on the three variables in the model, with each measurement item for the three variables corresponding to a survey question. Imagine the survey questions are as follows (the example is taken from a real survey-based study of system use, which you can read here [2]):

Please rate your agreement to the following statements on a scale from 1 (Strongly Disagree) to 7 (Strongly Agree):

Perceived Ease of Use
PEOU1: It has been easy for me to become skillful at using the Promotion Planning system.
PEOU2: I find the Promotion Planning system easy to use.
PEOU3: Learning to use the Promotion Planning system has been easy for me.

Perceived Usefulness
PU1: I find the Promotion Planning system useful for my job.
PU2: Using the Promotion Planning system helps me accomplish work tasks more quickly.

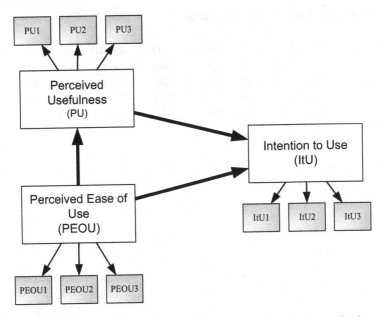

Fig. 4.2 Technology Acceptance Model [1] with measurement items in the smaller *boxes*

PU3: Using the Promotion Planning system increases my productivity.

Intention to Use
ItU1: My intention is to continue using the system to organize planning of promo-
tional items.
ItU2: I plan to continue using the system to organize planning of promotional items.
ItU3: I will continue using the current system to organize planning of promotional
items.

After the survey, the data collected could look like that shown in Table 4.1, with
a score between 1 and 7 for each respondent and each survey question.

Structural equation modeling involves specifying the equations that involve all
the measurement items and the variables they represent and then running an
algorithm that seeks one or more solutions to the problem of finding parameters
that fit the set of equations. We provide details about how this works in Sect. 4.3
below.

When we do structural equation modeling, we first estimate the measurement
model, the statistical model that links the latent variables to their measurement
items but does not consider the structural relationships between the variables
themselves (which we call path modeling). In other words, the measurement
model allows us to determine whether a group of measurable items (e.g., a set of
survey questions) converge sufficiently to estimate underlying and hard-to-measure

Table 4.1 Excerpt of survey data for the example

Survey respondent	PU1	PU2	PU3	PEOU1	PEOU2	PEOU3	ItU1	ItU2	ItU3
1	7.00	7.00	7.00	3.00	2.00	3.00	5.00	5.00	4.00
2	2.00	3.00	1.00	2.00	2.00	1.00	2.00	4.00	3.00
3	6.00	6.00	5.00	7.00	7.00	7.00	7.00	7.00	7.00
4	4.00	5.00	5.00	6.00	6.00	6.00	6.00	4.00	6.00
...	...	...	...	...	...	...	...	...	...

Fig. 4.3 Technology Acceptance Model [1] measurement model

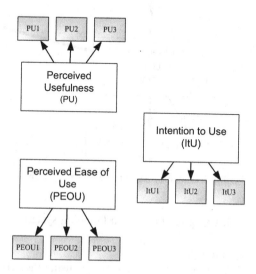

latent variables (e.g., talent or happiness). A measurement model for the TAM example could look like that shown in Fig. 4.3.

If the measurement model estimation is successful and we can clearly discern and identify three latent constructs, we then proceed to estimate the structural model—the relationships between the variables in the research model, that is, the hypotheses. A typical result from this step for the TAM example is shown in Fig. 4.4.

The example results shown in Fig. 4.4 indicate that the SEM can explain 31 % of the shared variance in Intention to use and 28 % of the shared variance in Perceived usefulness. We cannot explain Perceived ease of use because we have no equations that involve this concept as a dependent variable; it is only a predictor in this model. The model results also state that the influence of Perceived usefulness on Intent to use is 0.57 units, the average amount by which the dependent variable (Intent to use) increases when the independent variable (Perceived usefulness) increases by one unit while all other independent variables are held constant.

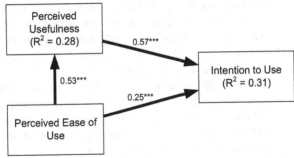

Fig. 4.4 Technology Acceptance Model [1] sample SEM results. *Source*: [3]

4.2 When Do We Use Structural Equation Models?

SEMs are statistical data analysis techniques that, like regression models and ANOVAs, belong to the class of procedures called general linear model. Their defining characteristic is the presence of multiple regression equations, such that the outcome of one equation is used as a predictor in another (set of) regression equations.

When are such models required? As with any other data analysis procedure, you can use SEMs to analyze data gathered through any quantitative research method, such as simulations, surveys, experiments, and archival data.

There are typically a number of conditions you can use to gauge whether to use SEMs for data analysis:

(a) The objective of the study is confirmatory rather than exploratory in nature. SEMs require one or more hypotheses, which they represent as a model, operationalize by means of measurement items, and then test statistically. The assumptions about "causal logic"[1] embedded in the model often have falsifiable implications that can be tested against the data. While the initial hypotheses often require model adjustment in light of empirical evidence, SEMs are rarely used for exploration only.

(b) The research model that specifies the hypotheses is complex, involving multiple associations between multiple independent and multiple dependent variables, and it usually has mediating and/or moderating variables (see Sect. 4.5).

(c) The research model involves latent concepts, that is, concepts that are not directly measurable abstractions from a phenomenon that relates to a real thing but is not tangible. Latent concepts are common in social sciences and include such examples as usefulness, time, satisfaction, and enjoyment. We all have

---

[1]Causal logic should not be equated with causality. SEMs do not prove causality per se. At best, causality can be approached using SEM if and when the design of the study is appropriate. We discuss the issue of examining causality in data in more detail in Chap. 7.

some understanding what is meant by these concepts but they are not real and not tangible—we cannot grasp, or measure them directly. This typically means that latent concepts are operationalized as multi-dimensional constructs—constructs that have several dimensions of meaning, and thus require multiple measurement items to capture.[2]

(d) Although this is a simplistic view, structural equation modeling is often associated with explanatory *survey* research, largely because surveys are a suitable research method to gather data on complex research models that include latent variables. Structural equation modeling is also used in experiments and other study designs.

It is useful to think about the type of research question you have in order to determine whether to use structural equation modeling as a data analysis strategy. SEMs can provide answers to three types of questions:

1. How much variance in the dependent variables does the model explain? The ability to test how much variance independent variables explain is useful for research questions like "what factors drive technology acceptance?" and "what are antecedents of user satisfaction?"
2. What is the directionality of the independent variables' effects on the dependent variables? In other words, are the effects positive (e.g., the results in Fig. 4.4) or negative? The ability to explain directionality is useful in answering research questions like "what is the impact of resistance to change on process improvement success?" and "how does information quality affect system success?"
3. What is the strength and the significance of the effects? The strength is expressed in the path weight, a decimal ranging between 0.00 and 1.00, while the significance is commonly expressed in the form of asterisks that denote certain p-values. For example, *** usually means $p < 0.001$, ** indicates $p < 0.01$, and * means $p < 0.05$. Paths that are not significant at least $p < 0.05$ are sometimes marked with the denotation ns (not significant). The ability to determine effects' strength and significance is useful in answering research questions like "do personality variables affect systems' implementation success more than organizational variables do?"

Many studies contain hypotheses or questions that combine these three types. For example, a hypothesis might read something like "Process modelers' perceived usefulness of a process modeling grammar is positively associated with their intention to continue using the grammar" [8]. The corresponding SEM would be expected:

(a) to explain much of the shared variance in intent to continue using a grammar through a model that includes perceived usefulness (point 1 above);

---

[2]Information on the intricacies of construct development is available in [4–7].

(b) to show that the path directionality between perceived usefulness and intent to continue using a grammar is positive (point 2 above);

(c) to show that the path is significant at least at $p < 0.05$ (point 3 above).

4.3 How Do We Examine Structural Equation Models?

In what follows, as elsewhere in this book, we assume that you have developed a research model with hypotheses, created suitable measurement instruments to measure all variables, and collected data that is now available in a format similar to that shown in Table 4.1. If that is the case, structural equation modeling usually consists of a five-step process:

1. **Model specification:** Specification of an a-priori research model with theoretical constructs and hypothesized relationships between them (i.e., the structural model)
2. **Model identification:** Estimation of unknown parameters (such as factor loadings, path coefficients, and explained variance) based on observed correlations or covariances
3. **Model estimation:** Finding of one set of model parameters that best fits the data
4. **Model fit testing:** Assessment of how well a model fits the data
5. **Model re-specification:** Improvement of either model parsimony or fit

Model specification, a conceptual task, relates to theory-building and construct development [4, 5, 9, 10], rather than to statistical procedures or knowledge. Since model specification is not the focus of this book, we assume that such a model was specified in order to design a measurement instrument, a data collection protocol, or gather any meaningful data to analyze. The outcome of this stage is a specified structural model, which means that the latent variables are arranged in a nomological network ([11], Chap. 4) and linked to their measurement items, as illustrated in Fig. 4.2

Arranging the latent variables in a nomological network means providing a graphic representation of the constructs in the research model and classifying them as *independent*, *dependent*, *mediating*, or *moderating* variables (see Fig. 4.5) based on the role they play in the research model.

Linking our latent variables to their measurement items, as illustrated in Fig. 4.2, refers to operationalizing the constructs in a set of measurement items. The challenge in this step is to guarantee *shared meaning* [12] between constructs and measurement items (e.g., the survey questions). If you fail to ensure shared meaning between the theoretical constructs and their operationalizations in the measurement variables, you will be limited in your ability to measure the constructs empirically.

Model identification, the first structural equation modeling task, is done using one of the many available structural equation modeling packages, such as WarpPLS, SmartPLS, LISREL, AMOS, and R or any other statistical software

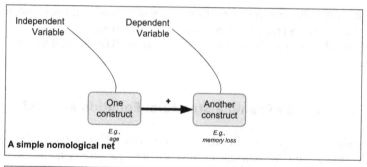

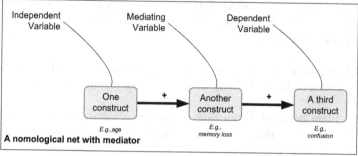

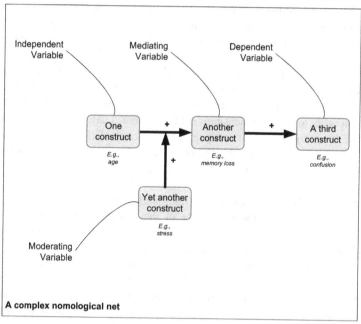

Fig. 4.5 Independent, dependent, mediating, and moderating variables (adapted from [11])

that supports structural equation modeling. We discuss some relevant implications concerning tool choice in Sect. 4.5.

During model identification, we determine whether the statistical software can "find" our specified model in the data we provide (e.g., a database such as that in Table 4.1). The software tries to identify values for all unknown parameters (e.g., factor loadings, error terms, path weights, shared variance) by examining statistical properties of the data provided. (Think of it as finding a theoretical model in a real model of data.) The software usually identifies these values by computing the correlations or covariances between all variables in the data and then relating these "real" correlations or covariances to the hypothesized correlations or covariances stipulated in the research model. For instance, in the TAM example, the research model stipulates strong correlations between Perceived usefulness and Intention to use. During model identification, the software searches for such correlations based on the data provided for the specified variables.

Figure 4.6 shows a general specified model and signifies all unknown parameters, including:

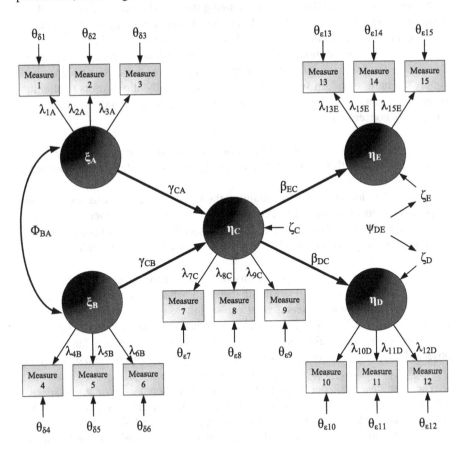

Fig. 4.6 Unknown parameters in model identification and estimation

- Error terms associated with each measurement item (Θ)
- Loadings for each measurement item on its latent construct (λ)
- Path weights between latent constructs (γ and β)
- Shared correlations between constructs (ϕ)
- The value of a latent independent construct (ξ)
- Shared variances of mediating and dependent constructs (η)
- Error terms of mediating and dependent constructs (ζ)
- Shared error terms between constructs (ψ)

The meaning of each of these parameters is well explained in books like [13], but it suffices for our purposes to understand that the software tries to find *any one model* where it can assign values (usually decimals between 0 and 1) to these parameters, as if it cannot do that, it cannot identify any solution for the specified model, and the specified model must be wrong. If that is the case, we have two options: We can change the model specification by inserting or deleting variables, inserting or deleting measurement items, changing the associations between measurement items and variables, and/or changing the associations between variables (viz., changing the nomological net). After each change, we can again try to identify the model in the data, until it works (we hope). A second option is based on getting the software to find the model in the data—that is, to find a needle in a haystack. Sometimes the software will not find a model that relates to the data because it is simply too hard to find. In such cases, the software usually allows users to alter the parameters related to the model identification (the search) process, including parameters concerning

- where to look (by promoting some variables as a starting point for a search),
- how long to look (how many iterations the algorithm should do before aborting), and
- where not to look (through constraining the search space by fixing some of the parameters to values like "1"). Constraining the search space reduces the number of unknown parameters to estimate, but it can be dangerous because we are making assumptions about relationships that may or may not be valid.

Clearly, SEM does not magically answer your research question; it is just an algorithm trying to find a relationship between what is in the data (observed correlations or covariance) versus what you said there would be (in your structural model). SEM usually fails to identify a model when the structural model (and thus our theory) does not make sense, that is, when it bears no resemblance to the observed structure in the data. However, failure to identify a model could also stem from other problems, all of which need inspection.

The first case, of course, is that the specified model is wrong and needs adjustment: must all the paths between the latent concepts look as you have specified, or could there be other paths between concepts? (The answer to this question depends on theory, not on data.) Are there other possible interpretations or theoretical arguments that suggest different linkages?

The second case is that the specified structural model is plausible, but the measurement model is too weak: the relationships between observable measurement items and latent concepts are not strong enough to support the reasoning about the relationships between the latent concepts. Here, the issue is empirical: the data is not good enough to test the theory.

Model estimation is where the real magic happens. During model identification, the software tries to find any one model that fits the data by identifying any one set of values for all unknown parameters. Because model identification is an estimation procedure (done using algorithms like maximum likelihood, partial least squares, or weighted least squares), the resulting model may not be one that best fits the data. Therefore, during model estimation, the software tries to find one set of model parameters that best fits the data, given a particular fit function that states which global variable to maximize (or minimize) in order to contrast multiple possible solutions.

The reason for this step is that structural equation modeling, much like the process related to any other general linear model, is a procedure in which we estimate a likely solution to a set of equations; we guess values for parameters without having enough data to solve all the equations. Therefore, statistically, the models are almost always under-specified, and any one set of structural equations can yield multiple solutions that solve all equations. Model estimation seeks the best model. A simple example that is quite common is that the fit function is based on the shared variance of the key dependent variable (say, Intention to use in our example), so the software runs an algorithm to "estimate all unknown parameters such that R^2 (Intention to use) is maximized." Of course, the fit function is not at all simple, which bring us to the next step.

Model fit testing involves the statistical software's computing a number of goodness-of-fit indices that serve as approximations for the question, "how well does my model fit the data?" Given the "true" (unobservable) relationships in the underlying population, the specified SEM estimates whether the sampled data gets close to mimicking or explaining the "true" unobservable structure, expressed through the covariance matrix that is estimated ex-ante. Measures of goodness of fit typically summarize the discrepancy between observed values and the values expected under the model in question. The rationale behind this step is the ambition of a study to explain a phenomenon; in other words, we are trying to build and evaluate theoretical models that explain real-world observations. Under the assumption that the real-world data (say, our survey responses) are real and correct, achieving this ambition requires finding a theoretical model that specifies equations that can perfectly describe all the real data—which usually means correctly estimating all the correlations or covariances between all of the variables.

As with any of the other steps, there are many ways to describe or evaluate "model fit." Measurements (or indices) for model fit have been developed that describe some statistic or other to characterize how well a model fits a set of data. Because these measurements, as any other statistic, have several advantages and disadvantages, we are confronted with a variety of goodness-of-fit indices.[3]

---

[3]For more information on the various fit indices, see [14].

Table 4.2 Goodness-of-fit indices with results for the models, as studied in [3]

Fit index	Suggested value	Specified models		
		TAM	ECT	Hybrid
GFI	>0.900	0.942	0.932	0.926
AGFI	>0.900	0.933	0.913	0.901
NFI	>0.900	0.956	0.932	0.915
NNFI	>0.900	0.946	0.923	0.905
CFI	>0.900	0.964	0.943	0.927
SRMR	<0.050	0.0439	0.0489	0.0496
RMSEA	<0.080	0.0731	0.0742	0.0784
χ^2 (df, p)	–	119.383 (24, 0.00)	292.705 (49, 0.00)	537.519 (81, 0.00)
R^2 for ItU	–	0.310	0.151	0.355

Table 4.2 reports on some of the most common indices and contrasts them for three types of specified theoretical models—TAM, Expectation-Confirmation Theory (ECT), and a Hybrid model—that all explain a particular phenomenon (in this case: continued usage intentions by some users of some tool). Table 4.2 provides statistics with which to evaluate which of the models fits the reality it tries to explain best. In this particular case, the Hybrid model is best, because:

- the dependent variable's R^2 value is highest,
- it meets the suggested threshold values for all fit indices (GFI, AGFI, NFI, NNFI, CFI), and
- it meets the suggested threshold values for the residual error (SRMR, RMSEA).

Generally speaking, goodness of fit indices broadly fall into four classes of indices [14]:

- Discrepancy functions, such as the χ^2 test or the relative chi square test (which divides χ^2 by the degrees of freedom in the model). Discrepancy functions are traditional, interesting, but also potentially misleading test statistics: they measure how close the model is to the underlying data. Rejecting the null hypothesis) ("there is no difference between the estimated model and the real data") implies poor model fit, whereas failing to reject the null-hypothesis implies a good fit. The latter is one of the rare instances in which we can celebrate lack of statistical significance. As with any other statistic, the χ^2 test is difficult to interpret and potentially misleading, so we should report it only together with other tests of model fit.
- Tests that compare the target model with the null model, such as the CFI, NFI, GFI, and NNFI tests.
- Information theory goodness-of-fit measures, such as the AIC, BCC, BIC, and CAIC.
- Non-centrality fit measures, such as the NCP.

The outcome of this stage indicates how well the model fits the data. Ideally, we'll have high values on our goal function (such as shared variance in our dependent variables) and acceptable values for the goodness-of-fit indices, in which case, we have completed the model specification. However, in most (if not all) cases, these high values are unlikely to be achieved the first time we run structural equation modeling, which leads us to the final step.

Model re-specification goes back to the first stage, model specification, to specify a better model. "Better" may mean a model that fits the data better (i.e., that scores higher during model-fit testing), a model that achieves higher shared variance results for dependent variables, or a more parsimonious model that requires fewer variables, measurement items, and/or associations between variables to achieve similar results and fit. This last part is based on the argument that more parsimonious theoretical models are better, as they offer a simpler, more elegant explanation for observations [10]. Re-specification requires redoing the entire process of structural equation modeling until an acceptable solution is found. Some statistical software (e.g., LISREL) provide modification indices that suggest where and how to change a structural model to achieve better fit to the data. Independent of whether the software you use provides such assistance, the key challenge is conceptual rather than empirical: does the re-specified model make sense—or make more sense than the old model—given what you are trying to explain and how you are trying to explain it?

4.4 How Do We Report Structural Equation Model Analyses?

A number of guidelines exist that relate to the honest and faithful reporting of structural equation modeling results in academic publications. In a nutshell, the idea is to present sufficient information so readers can re-conduct or evaluate the steps undertaken during the computation. In other words, it should be possible to compute the same results without having access to the original data.

In most publications, reporting is done in two stages: measurement model results and structural model results. In some cases, supplementary or post-hoc analyses are also reported (typically in appendices) that provide even more insights into the data or results based on additional statistical procedures.

Guidelines for reporting results vary over time—sometimes quite drastically—so check for new reporting guidelines regularly. Currently, several guidelines govern the reporting of measurement model and structural models [5–7, 15–20].

1. Measurement Model Reporting
Examinations of measurement models evaluate whether the model of what is measured fits the properties of the data collected. The typical criteria are validity and reliability, which are also called the psychometric properties of measurement variables. Validity and reliability describe the benchmarks against which the adequacy and accuracy (and, ultimately, the quality) of quantitative method procedures are evaluated in scientific research. Reliability describes the extent to

which a variable or set of variables is consistent in what it intends to measure, while validity describes whether the data collected measure what the researcher set out to measure. Tests that can demonstrate validity and reliability include:

- Uni-dimensionality: A construct is uni-dimensional if its constituent items represent one underlying trait
- Reliability and composite reliability: Reliability refers to the degree to which scale items (reliability) and constructs (composite reliability) are free from error and, therefore, yield consistent results.
- Convergent validity: Convergent validity tests whether measures that should be related are related.
- Discriminant validity: Discriminant validity refers to the degree to which the items that measure different constructs are mutually exclusive.

Any of the available structural equation modeling software packages offers these tests and others. Threshold values are constantly being updated, but they generally conform to the norms described here [16].

Common practice is to include the following tables to summarize model measurement results:

- Scale properties: a table that lists all measurement items, their means, standard deviations, item loadings, and loading significances.
- Construct properties: a table that lists all variables (i.e., latent constructs), their means, standard deviations, Cronbach's α, composite reliability p_c, and average variance extracted (AVE).
- Construct and item correlations: tables that show all correlations between (i) latent constructs and (ii) all measurement items. These tables are often placed in appendices because they can be large.

2. Structural Model Reporting

Representations in reports on structural model results vary from tabular to graphic models. Graphic results (as shown in Fig. 4.4) are often preferable because they facilitate straightforward inspection of both the results and their implications regarding the hypotheses expressed in the research model.

Common reporting practices include specifications of all shared-variance results for all mediating or dependent variables, weight and significance for each path between the constructs, and all common goodness-of-fit indices. Table 4.2 gives one such example, but results can also be given in plain text, such as that shown in [21]: "Goodness of fit statistics for the structural model (GFI = 0.81, NFI = 0.90, NNFI = 0.91, CFI = 0.92, SRMR = 0.041, RMSEA = 0.07, $\chi 2 = 2807.65$, df = 740, $\chi 2/\text{df} = 3.79$) suggest acceptable approximate fit of the model to the [...] data set." In this example, the "best" structural model does not achieve all recommended values for the various indices because the goodness-of-fit tests showed some violations of the recommended thresholds (in this case, the guidelines [22]).

The rule to follow in these cases is simple: report *all* results on the indices, even if a threshold is not met. Empirical science is never perfect, and we should not pretend otherwise. Good reporting means faithfully and openly reporting actual results from a data collection and analysis effort so readers can gauge the quality of the results (and the trustworthiness of any conclusions) for themselves. In the absence of such results (e.g., for goodness-of-fit tests), readers do not know whether results can be trusted, so they don't trust them. Readers with at least some familiarity with quantitative research know that the reality of data collection and analysis does not always meet the standards set out in theory, so results and implications are often found to be acceptable within the boundaries of their limitations, but only when such "problematic incidents" are reported.

4.5 What If...

This section briefly addresses some advanced questions and topics around structural equation modeling.

What If I Have Mediation Effects in My SEM?
Variables in a research model can be independent, dependent or mediating. A mediating variable, in a sense, is both independent and dependent.

The challenge with mediating variables is knowing whether they do in fact mediate anything. Figure 4.7 illustrates three alternative models for the TAM, including two that show Perceived usefulness's partial and full mediation of Perceived ease of use's effect on Intention to use.

All three models shown in Fig. 4.7 are theoretically and statistically possible, and all three models make sense. Therefore, when testing SEMs that include mediation between variables, it is good practice to examine the type of mediation effect that is present using any of several procedures [23–25]. These procedures estimate all three variants of relationships a, b, and c between three variables (Fig. 4.7) and, using a fit function, determine which of the variants best explains the data. At present, the recommended procedure is that by Zhao [25], which distinguishes five types of mediation:

1. No effect: Neither the interaction term a × b nor the path c is significant, so there is no effect whatsoever, direct or indirect.
2. Direct-only: The interaction term a × b is not significant, but the path c is significant. There is no mediation, as only the direct paths are significant.
3. Indirect-only: The interaction term a × b is significant, but the path c is insignificant. This is a form of full mediation in which there are no direct effects (e.g., of Perceived ease of use on Intent to use), but all effects are fully mediated (e.g., through Perceived usefulness).
4. Competitive: The interaction term a × b and the path c are significant, and the term a × b × c is not positive. Therefore, there are both a mediated effect (a × b) and a direct effect (c), but these two effects point in opposite directions. (For

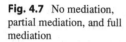

Fig. 4.7 No mediation, partial mediation, and full mediation

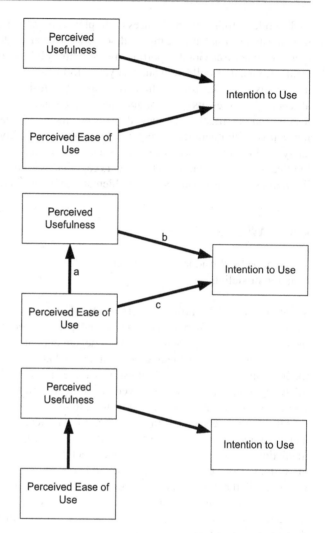

example, the direct effect of Perceived ease of use adds to Intent to use, but the mediated effect through Perceived usefulness detracts from Intent to use.)

Complementary: The interaction term a × b and the path c are significant, and the term a × b × c is positive. Therefore, there are both a mediated effect (a × b) and a direct effect (c), and these two effects point in the same direction, complementing each other (see Fig. 4.7).

The Zhao procedure [25] is a simple macro that can be run in standard statistics software like SPSS and SAS [26] and downloaded from the web.[4]

---

[4]http://afhayes.com/spss-sas-and-mplus-macros-and-code.html

Fig. 4.8 Example of a
moderation effect

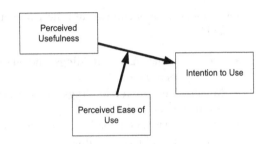

What If I Have Moderation Effects in My SEM?

Moderation is a challenging effect conceptually and statistically. Consider the
model shown in Fig. 4.8, which can be read to suggest that Perceived usefulness
determines Intention to use (so far, so good) and that Perceived ease of use
moderates the strength of the relationship between Perceived usefulness and Intention to use. Thus, the effect of Perceived usefulness on Intention to use might be
stronger if the levels of Perceived ease of use are high, and weaker if the levels are
low. In other words, moderation occurs when the relationship between two
variables depends on a third variable or when the effect of one predictor on a
dependent variable differs at different values of the second predictor.

Moderation is a type of interaction effect that comes into play when we want to
learn how two variables A and B interact (A × B) in effecting a third, dependent
variable C. This is how moderations are analyzed in AN(C)OVA procedures. In
structural equation modeling, examining a potential moderation in a research model
typically involves testing and comparing two SEMs: one for the sub-sample in
which the values for the moderator are low against the sub-sample in which the
values for the moderator are high. The trick here is to split the research data into two
sub-samples based on the moderator's values. For example, if the moderator were
"gender," the two sub-samples would be all male and all female. If the moderator is
not a binary or categorical but, say, a continuous variable (such as ratings for
Perceived ease of use), two binary variables, "high" and "low," can differentiate
the sub-samples. Then the same SEM is estimated for two data sets (the two
sub-samples).

The challenge is to identify the differences between the two models, which can
be tricky because many things differ in two SEMs: the shared variance in a
dependent variable, the path weights and significance, the factor loadings of
measurement items to variables, error terms, shared error terms, and so forth. We
want to determine, then, whether the differences between the two models are
differences in things we are interested in—particularly shared variance in a dependent variable, path weights, and significance; differences in things that are problematic, particularly error terms and shared error terms; or both.

The procedure described in [27, 28] suggests five steps:

1. For each moderator, split the data sample into two groups (high/low) and
   compare the SEMs across the two sub-samples.

2. Once model 1 is identified, use the parameters from this model to constrain model 2:

   - Model 2a has **factor loadings** and **error variances** *constrained* to the parameters of model 1.
   - Model 2b has **factor loadings** *free* but **error variances** *constrained* to the parameters of model 1.
   - Model 2c has **factor loadings** and **error variances** *free*.
   - Model 2d has **factor loadings** *constrained* to the parameters of model 1 but **error variances** *free*.

Thus, we estimate five structural models and then evaluate the relative chi-square by comparing the differences in chi-square to differences in degrees of freedom (viz., $\Delta\chi^2/\Delta df$):

3. Compare model 2b to 2c: if there is a significant difference it is caused by error variances, so the differences between models 1 and 2 are caused by measurement error, not a moderation effect.
4. Compare model 2a to 2b: if there is a significant difference it is caused by different factor loadings and path coefficients, so the differences between models 1 and 2 are caused by a moderation effect.
5. If the differences between models 2a and 2b and between 2b and 2c are both significant, there is moderation and error variance. In this case, shared error correlations (φ and ψ) must be set to invariant in another set of models (2e and 2f) to extract true moderation effects.

This procedure is precise but also cumbersome, so a second procedure that is more popular because it is simpler to compute and interpret has been proposed: multi-group analysis. This procedure works according to the same principle of comparing the same SEM against two sub-samples based on levels of the moderator (high versus low, or different categories of a nominal variable), but the analysis is restricted to comparing the parameters for the paths in the structural model across the models estimated for two groups. In other words, multi-group analysis tests whether $\beta(1) \neq \beta(2)$ for the paths in the various models. For example, imagine the moderator is "experience with technology." Assume we estimate the TAM for experienced users get the results β (Perceived usefulness $\rightarrow$ Intention to use) = 0.45 for the experienced group, and $\beta = 0.14$ for the inexperienced group. The analysis then tests whether the difference $\beta(1) - \beta(2) = 0.31$ is significant given the data (sample size, loadings, error terms). The procedure is implemented in many of the current software packages (e.g., SmartPLS) and described in [18, 29–31].

What If I Have Formative Measurement Items in My SEM?

This chapter made a key assumption: that the relationship between variables in a SEM (the constructs) and the measurement items is reflective, that is, that the construct is reflected in its measures. In formative measurement, another way to

Formative Construct **Reflective Construct**

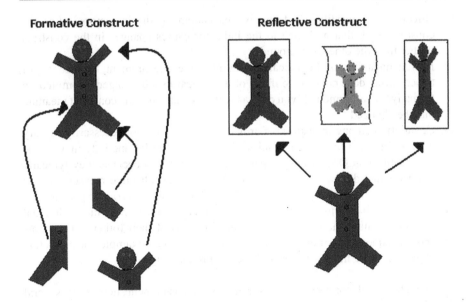

Fig. 4.9 Formative and reflective measurement

measure constructs, the meaning of the construct is determined ("formed") by its empirical indicators.

Let's take the variable "firm performance" as an example. We can create a reflective scale that measures top managers' views of how well the firm is performing. These measurement items can be interchangeable so the researcher can assess the measures' reliability in reflecting the construct. Alternatively, we can create a set of metrics for firm performance that measure elements like ROI, profitability, return on equity, and market share. These items are not interchangeable, so they are formative. Figure 4.9 illustrates the distinction.

Any construct can be measured reflectively or formatively, as constructs are not necessarily (inherently) reflective or formative. However, the choice of measurement has implications for structural equation modeling because it changes how we can evaluate whether the measurement model is "good" (and, thus, how we can identify a structural model).

Handling reflective and/or formative models is an intricate issue that is often debated. However, some heuristics can help you identify which type of measurement is most appropriate for a given construct [19]. For the constructs of your choice, we recommend that you try to gain conceptual clarity on how your indicators relate to the constructs, and then test your conceptions for direction of causality, interchangeability of the indicators, covariation among indicators, and variations in nomological nets.

1. Direction of causality—In formative measurement, the indicators define the construct such that a change in the indicator causes changes in the construct (rather than the other way around).
2. Interchangeability of the indicators—In reflective measurement, the meaning of the construct does not change if any of the indicators are changed or omitted. In formative measurement, if you drop a formative indicator, the construct meaning may be changed.
3. Covariation among indicators—Formative measures do not necessarily co-vary with one another (e.g., the variables Market share and Productivity may not be correlated in an Organizational performance construct) because they typically cover distinct dimensions of meaning. However, in reflective measurement, a high degree of covariation (e.g., in indices like Cronbach's α) is expected.
4. Variations in nomological nets—For formative measures, the individual indicators within the construct may vary in terms of their (other) antecedents and consequences. For instance, in the firm performance example, the predictors of Market share may differ from those for Productivity.

The choice of formative versus reflective measurement items has several implications for structural equation modeling, as reliability is more difficult to determine for formative constructs. Cronbach's α as a measure becomes effectively meaningless, and a multicollinearity assessment is required (e.g., on basis of VIFs). In addition, during the specification of a model that includes formative constructs, different models should be tested based on varying uses of exogenous items (i.e., the measurement items) and then compared to find the "best" model. Finally, model fit indices often assume entirely reflective measurement models. In other words, they may not be meaningful (or cannot be computed) for formative models, and alternative measures will be required [32].

What If I Don't Know Which Software to Use?
A final decision that is often challenging for researchers is the choice of software. Obviously, the decision is influenced by availability, price, documentation, and so forth, but in structural equation modeling, the choice of software is further complicated by the availability of two classes of software packages that implement two types of structural equation modeling: correlation-based versus covariance-based. Most researchers equate this difference to the difference between partial least squares (PLS) modeling versus covariance-based modeling. Covariance-based modeling packages are older and thus more established, but PLS modeling packages are not only newer and very popular, but often also available free or at lower cost and are often more intuitive and easier to use. Table 4.3 summarizes additional differences.

When a typical reflective measurement model is used, covariance-based structural equation modeling is usually preferred because its procedures, indices, and tests are rigorous, well-developed, and precise. However, correlation-based modeling should be used in several cases [20]:

Table 4.3 Correlation-based versus covariance-based software packages for structural equation modeling

Criterion	Correlation-based modeling (e.g., SmartPLS, PLSGraph)	Covariance-based modeling (e.g., LISREL, AMOS, MPlus)
Objective	Prediction-oriented	Parameter-oriented
Distribution Assumptions	Non-parametric and normal	Normal distribution (parametric)
Required sample size	Small (from about 30–100)[a]	Large (usually above 100)[a]
Model complexity	Large models are okay	Large models (50+ indicator variables) are problematic
Parameter Estimates	Potential bias	Stable if assumptions are met
Indicators per construct	Few indicators are okay. Large number is okay	Typically a minimum of 3–4 to meet identification requirements
Statistical tests for parameter estimates	Inference requires bootstrapping or jack-knifing	Assumptions must be met, then F-tests
Measurement model	Can handle both formative and reflective indicators	Can typically handle only reflective models
Goodness-of-fit measures	None or few	Many

[a]Do not take these ranges as a fixed criterion. The required sample size depends, amongst others, on the number of constructs and thus the number of parameters to be estimated in the model

- When the data is non-normally distributed—Correlation-based modeling imposes fewer restrictions on the distribution because correlation always implies a standardization.
- When the model includes formative measures—Covariance-based modeling packages are (so far) rather ill-equipped to compute or evaluate formative models.
- When the research model is highly complex—Often in these cases, correlation-based modeling is more stable, so the software does not crash as often.
- When the research objective is exploration or prediction—Some researchers argue that the validation principles (and the strict quality criteria) of covariance-based modeling are not fully applicable to these research objectives.

References

1. Davis FD (1989) Perceived usefulness, perceived ease of use, and user acceptance of information technology. MIS Q 13:319–340
2. Recker J (2016) Reasoning about discontinuance of information system use. J Inf Technol Theory Appl 17:101–126
3. Recker J (2010) Explaining usage of process modeling grammars: comparing three theoretical models in the study of two grammars. Inf Manage 47:316–324
4. Lewis BR, Templeton GF, Byrd TA (2005) A methodology for construct development in MIS research. Eur J Inf Syst 14:388–400

5. MacKenzie SB, Podsakoff PM, Podsakoff NP (2011) Construct measurement and validation procedures in MIS and behavioral research: integrating new and existing techniques. MIS Q 35:293–334
6. Straub DW (1989) Validating instruments in MIS research. MIS Q 13:147–169
7. Straub DW, Boudreau M-C, Gefen D (2004) Validation guidelines for IS positivist research. Commun Assoc Inf Syst 13:380–427
8. Recker J (2010) Continued use of process modeling grammars: the impact of individual difference factors. Eur J Inf Syst 19:76–92
9. Hirschheim R (2008) Some guidelines for the critical reviewing of conceptual papers. J Assoc Inf Syst 9:432–441
10. Weber R (2012) Evaluating and developing theories in the information systems discipline. J Assoc Inf Syst 13:1–30
11. Recker J (2012) Scientific research in information systems: a beginner's guide. Springer, Berlin
12. Burton-Jones A, Lee AS (2011) Thinking about measures and measurement. In: Sprague RH Jr (ed) Proceedings of the 44th Hawaii international conference on system sciences. IEEE Computer Society, Kauai, HI, pp 1–10
13. Jöreskog KG, Sörbom D (2001) LISREL 8: user's reference guide. Scientific Software International, Lincolnwood, IL
14. Moss S (2009) Fit indices for structural equation modeling. Psychlopedia. http://www.psych-it.com.au/Psychlopedia/article.asp?id=277
15. Boudreau M-C, Gefen D, Straub DW (2001) Validation in information systems research: a state-of-the-art assessment. MIS Q 25:1–16
16. Gefen D, Rigdon EE, Straub DW (2011) An update and extension to SEM guidelines for administrative and social science research. MIS Q 35:iii–xiv
17. Gefen D, Straub DW, Boudreau M-C (2000) Structural equation modeling and regression: guidelines for research practice. Commun Assoc Inf Syst 4:1–77
18. Hair JF, Hult GTM, Ringle CM, Sarstedt M (2013) A primer on Partial Least Squares Structural Equation Modeling (PLS-SEM). Sage, Thousand Oaks, CA
19. Petter S, Straub DW, Rai A (2007) Specifying formative constructs in IS research. MIS Q 31:623–656
20. Ringle CM, Sarstedt M, Straub DW (2012) Editor's comments: a critical look at the use of PLS-SEM in MIS quarterly. MIS Q 36:iii–xiv
21. Recker J, Rosemann M, Green P, Indulska M (2011) Do ontological deficiencies in modeling grammars matter? MIS Q 35:57–79
22. Im KS, Grover V (2004) The use of structural equation modeling in IS research: review and recommendations. In: Whitman ME, Woszczynski AB (eds) The handbook of information systems research. Idea Group, Hershey, PA, pp 44–65
23. Baron RM, Kenny DA (1986) The moderator-mediator variable distinction in social psychological research: conceptual, strategic, and statistical considerations. J Pers Soc Psychol 51:1173–1182
24. Sobel ME (1982) Asymptotic confidence intervals for indirect effects in structural equation models. Sociol Methodol 13:290–312
25. Zhao X, Lynch JG Jr, Chen Q (2010) Reconsidering Baron and Kenny: myths and truths about mediation analysis. J Consum Res 37:197–206
26. Preacher KJ, Hayes AF (2004) SPSS and SAS procedures for estimating indirect effects in simple mediation models. Behav Res Methods Instrum Comput 36:717–731
27. Dabholkar PA, Bagozzi RP (2002) An attitudinal model of technology-based self-service: moderating effects of consumer traits and situational factors. J Acad Mark Sci 30:184–201
28. Im I, Kim Y, Han H-J (2008) The effects of perceived risk and technology type on users' acceptance of technologies. Inf Manage 45:1–9

29. Henseler J, Chin WW (2010) A comparison of approaches for the analysis of interaction effects between latent variables using partial least squares path modeling. Struct Equ Model 17:82–109
30. Henseler J, Ringle CM, Sinkovics RR (2009) The use of partial least squares path modeling in international marketing. In: Sinkovics RR, Ghauri PN (eds) New challenges to international marketing. Advances in international marketing, vol 20. Emerald Group Publishing, Bingley, pp 277–319
31. Sarstedt M, Henseler J, Ringle CM (2011) Multi-group analysis in Partial Least Squares (PLS) path modeling: alternative methods and empirical results. In: Sarstedt M, Schwaiger M, Taylor CR (eds) Measurement and research methods in international marketing. Advances in international marketing, vol 22. Emerald Group Publishing, London, pp 195–218
32. Henseler J, Sarstedt M (2013) Goodness-of-fit indices for partial least squares path modeling. Comput Stat 28:565–580

Nested Data and Multilevel Models: Hierarchical Linear Modeling

5

Most of the people and cases that are subject to research in business and information systems are nested within hierarchies. A hierarchy attaches roles to certain levels and typically makes higher-level roles responsible for lower-level roles. At all levels of the organizational hierarchy, this approach translates into small clusters of managers and larger clusters of team members (which may include managers of lower-level teams). Such a hierarchy could range from a CEO and her team of executives to a line manager and his team of operators, but the hierarchy even continues beyond the organization, as organizations are nested within industries, industries within countries, and so on. Sometimes we want to study effects that cross these hierarchical layers. For example, we may be interested in the effect of managers' behavior on their team members' behavior, or the effect of remuneration policies at the level of the organization on individual performance and individual turnover intentions. In other words, we may want to study the effect of a variable that varies at the group level (i.e., between groups) on another variable that differs for every individual (i.e., it varies within groups). This kind of investigation calls for the use of hierarchical linear models.

5.1   What Are Hierarchical Linear Models?

Hierarchical linear models (HLMs) are models that allow relationships between variables both within and *across* multiple levels to be investigated. A level refers to the layer of a hierarchy at which we measure a certain variable (e.g., the individual level, the team level, the organizational level). Similar to the structural equation models (SEMs) discussed in Chap. 4, HLMs are a form of multivariate regression model. However, in addition to having (1) several dependent measures or variables and (2) dependent measures that can also appear as predictors for some other dependent variable, HLMs introduce (3) a way to *study relationships between data across multiple levels*, which is HLMs' defining feature.

© Springer International Publishing Switzerland 2017
W. Mertens et al., *Quantitative Data Analysis*, DOI 10.1007/978-3-319-42700-3_5

Because of the nature of hierarchies, investigating relationships that cross multiple levels requires both regressing independent variables on dependent variables and comparing groups so, in a way, we are combining regressions with ANOVA. As you will see later in this chapter, HLM has elements of regression, SEM, and ANOVA methods, and they can be used interchangeably with these methods in many situations.

For the purposes of this chapter, we use a simple example of a hierarchy: teachers and their classes of students. Imagine we want to study the effect of (a) teachers' expectations of how well their students will do at school, and (b) student IQ on (c) student performance. Student performance and IQ are personal—variables that differ for every student—so they are individual-level variables. Therefore, students are our level 1 units of analysis—the lowest hierarchical level in our data—and the effect of IQ on student performance has to be studied at that level. Teachers' expectations do not necessarily vary at the individual level, as students may have different teachers, and different teachers may have their own expectations for all of their students. For the sake of simplicity, let us assume that every class has a different teacher and that every teacher sets his own expectations for all of the students in his class. For example, some teachers think all students are dumb and will never achieve anything, while others think most of them will grow up to be Einsteins. Figure 5.1 represents this example graphically: it shows both the structure of the hierarchy and the hypothesized HLM.

Figure 5.1 also illustrates that hierarchical models deal with variables that differ *between all units* of analysis (e.g., IQ), variables that differ *between the groups* created by the hierarchy (e.g., teacher expectations), and variables that vary *both within and between groups* (e.g., student performance). Another way to explain this structure is that data is nested in terms of its units—students are nested in classes—so the assumption of independence of observations is violated (see Chap. 8) because

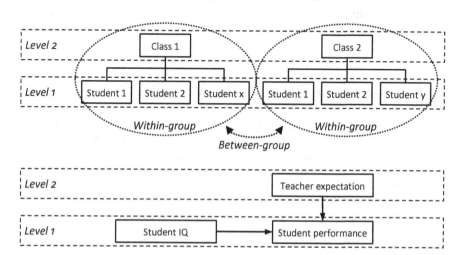

Fig. 5.1 Illustration of a multilevel hierarchy (*top*) and model (*bottom*)

units *within* the same group will be influenced by (upper-level) variables that differ *between* groups. As a result, the scores of level-1 units (students) will be less independent within groups than between groups.

Before HLM was developed, researchers couldn't deal well with this violation of assumptions, so one of two approaches was typically employed [1]. (In fact, both are still widely—and erroneously—employed.) The first approach was to aggregate individual-level variables to the group level (e.g., taking the class means for IQ and student performance) and to test the model at that group level (e.g., using a regression or SEM). The problem with this approach was that individual-level variance was lost—for example, we would lose the differences in IQ between any pair of students—so the estimation of effects was biased and power was reduced because the sample size (n) decreased (fewer classes than students). Apart from these technical problems, losing individual-level variance usually also means losing hard-earned and potentially useful data points and variance. Therefore, this approach is desirable only when the theorized relationships of interest are defined at an upper level of analysis (e.g., the effect of teacher expectations on average class performance), not when the unit of analysis is at a lower level, as in our working example.

The other approach was to assign group-level variables to individuals and evaluate the model at the lowest level (i.e., at the level of the students, not the class). Therefore, for example, all students in one class were assigned the same value for teacher evaluation. The problem with this approach was that it caused covariance between error terms, which again biased the estimation of effect sizes and caused all manner of other problems (see Chap. 7). This approach also violated the important assumption of independence that lends credibility to regression-based statistical methods (see Chap. 8).

The main advantage of HLM is that it accounts for (error) variance at both the individual level and the group level. It acknowledges that students in the same class do not have the same IQ or performance but do have the same teacher. Therefore, the assumption of independent error variances is not violated, but independent variables are still estimated at the appropriate level of analysis, and interdependence between individuals that are part of the same group is accounted for [2].

5.2   When Do We Use HLMs?

Generally speaking, HLM is used in situations similar to those in which SEM is used (see Chap. 4), with the important extra condition of studying nested data—that is, data in which not all observations are independent. More precisely, HLM is used to study how independent variables affect dependent variables within and across levels of nestedness, taking into account how these effects differ between groups at the lowest level of the nestedness hierarchy.

Nestedness can mean many things. This chapter focuses on hierarchically nested data (e.g., in organizational hierarchies), but HLM is applicable in another situation in which there is no full independence between units: longitudinal data. In longitudinal data, multiple measurements are taken from the same unit of analysis over time. Therefore, observations *within* these units can be *more* dependent than observations *between* the units over time. Although conceptually different, longitudinal data technically has the same nestedness as hierarchical data, as measurements are nested in units, and units are nested in groups of multiple units [1]. We saw in Chap. 2 that we can also use repeated-measures ANOVA to study this kind of data, and Chap. 6 introduces two models that are closely related to hierarchical models: fixed effect and random effect models. We discuss the differences between all these when we get into the nuts and bolts of HLM, but you could say that HLM is a *combination* of fixed-effects models and random-effect models [3].

Although the examples in this chapter have only one dependent variable and mutually exclusive groups, variants of HLM can also be used to study multiple dependent variables and data that contain "cross-classified" groups, where one unit of analysis can be part of multiple groups. For example, certain students in one class may attend selected courses in another class. In this case, some students, unlike others, belong to *two or more* classes. In Fig. 5.1, this overlap between classes would show certain students being linked to multiple classes. In such cases, since the standard HLM assumes that every unit is part of only one class, variants of HLM have to be used, to which researchers refer as cross-classified linear mixed modeling, cross-classified multilevel measurement modeling, or cross-classified random effects modeling. Garson [3] is an excellent starting point for learning more about these methods and Huta [4] is another good source for learning about when to use HLM.

5.3   How Do We Investigate HLMs?

The first step in investigating multilevel models is ensuring our data reflects the correct level of analysis and is reliable. The second step is, ironically, determining whether HLM is required using a simple ANOVA analysis. Then, if HLM is indeed required, we can test the multilevel hypotheses. We discuss each step in turn.

Aggregation and Measurement Reliability

Although it may sound like a silly thing to do, it is often necessary—or perhaps just preferable—to measure level-2 variables at level 1 and vice versa. For example, we could ask students (level 1) about their teacher (level 2), or we could ask managers (level 2) to rate the performance of each of their team members (level 1). Therefore, we sometimes need to make sure we can reliably attribute data to the intended level *before* evaluating whether the measurement itself is reliable. This check is necessary only when we measure a variable at a level other than the level at which we analyze it.

Attributing the data to the intended level may require *aggregating* the data to the right level. Aggregation can take many forms because we compute an aggregate statistic for individual data (e.g., taking the average of student performance per teacher). Aggregation means losing important variance, but only if that variance sits at the appropriate level. Consider an example: We want to know how a teacher is rated by her students. If we ask students to rate their teacher, and each of their ratings differs only marginally, the variance between students is not very informative, and aggregation (e.g., to an average for the whole class) is appropriate. However, if the students disagree about their teacher, the variance *would be* informative and *should be* kept. As this example shows, we need to evaluate the extent of agreement between students (i.e., to what degree their assessments of their teacher are similar) and the extent to which their scores are reliable and consistent. However, we may need to evaluate the extent of agreement, reliability, and consistency either before or after we aggregate items and evaluate scales—and this is where it can get a little confusing.

Peterson and Castro [5] described three aggregation strategies that we can use, depending on (1) where we theoretically *expect* most of the variation to lie (between level-1 students or between level-2 teachers) and (2) the level at which a variable was measured, that is, the level of the raters. These two conditions define the order in which we evaluate agreement, combine indicators into scales, and aggregate either the indicators or the scales to the appropriate level, depending on which aggregation came first. While Chap. 4 discussed how multiple indicator variables all represent one construct, HLM, much like regression, does not require variables to be measured in this way since we could have just one reliable direct measure—not a latent construct. However, if variables are measured using indicators we must "build" the constructs first, which usually consists of taking the average of all indicators. In Fig. 5.2, building a construct would mean taking the average of the three indicators that are attached to one construct within one unit and level. Taking the average of the construct measures of multiple units or the average of indicators of multiple units is aggregating scores to a different level. For our student-teacher example, we might assume that teacher expectations vary at the class level. In that case, we need first to evaluate the degree of the students' agreement about their teacher's expectations at the level of the indicators (the variables/items that measure teacher expectation), then take the average of all these student ratings (i.e., create one score per indicator/item per teacher), and only then combine the indicators into one construct score per teacher (pictured on the right in Fig. 5.2).

This approach is the one of the three approaches that Peterson and Castro [5] proposed that is most appropriate for our example. Other approaches (which

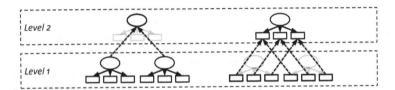

Fig. 5.2 Schematic illustration of aggregation across levels; each *oval* with three *squares* represents one construct and three indicators measured for one unit of analysis at the respective level of analysis

basically consist of executing the three steps in another order) are more appropriate in other circumstances.

Evaluating the agreement between students' ratings of their teachers' expectations ideally consists of evaluating within-group inter-rater agreement, the consistency of raters, and the reliability of group means. Within-group inter-rater agreement can be estimated using the r^*_{wg} coefficient, which indicates the degree to which raters in each group (class) agree, compared to completely random ratings [6]. The consistency of raters can be evaluated using a first variant of the Intraclass Correlation, the "ICC1 coefficient" [7]. ICC1 provides an estimate of how much of the variance in the data can be explained by the fact that there are groups. In other words, it compares the between-group variance to the sum of between- and within-group variance. This comparison can be calculated easily with an ANOVA procedure. Finally, the reliability of group means can be evaluated using another variant of Intraclass Correlations, the ICC2 coefficient [7]. ICC2 summarizes the amount of variance between groups minus the variance within groups as a proportion of the between-group variance. This calculation can also be done easily based on ANOVA results. These three indices are just a frequently used sample of many available indices and are by no means the only correct ones.

We realize that this explanation might be pretty confusing, so here is an excerpt of one of our own studies that illustrates the approach and gives you another example. This particular study measured leadership behaviors by asking team members questions about their leaders. Here is how we reported the data analysis:

> Before assessing the measurement reliability of the scales that measure leadership behavior, we assessed whether there was enough agreement to allow aggregation of the leadership behavior variables to the group level. Because measures of leadership behavior can theoretically be expected to vary more at the group level than at the individual level, we evaluated within-group agreement and intra-class correlations based on individual item scores before aggregating the items and creating group-level scales from aggregated items; that is, we used the CAS approach as described by Peterson and Castro [5]. We used the r^*_{wg} coefficient to assess within-group interrater agreement [6], and we used ICC1 and ICC2 to assess raters' consistency and the reliability of group means, respectively [7]. The ICC scores were derived from a one-way analysis of variance (ANOVA) on each of the variables of each scale, with the F tests' confirming that scores differed significantly between groups.
>
> Based on commonly accepted thresholds in multilevel research that relies on peer ratings in managerial jobs [7–9] and in line with previous research [10–12], we found good support for aggregating all items that measure the dimensions of empowering leadership behavior (average $r^*_{wg} = 0.71$; average $ICC1 = 0.17$ and $ICC2 = 0.44$; F (143, 435–440) ranging from 1.25 to 2.67 with all $p < 0.05$). Items were aggregated to the group level to form one reliable scale of overall empowering leadership (CFA in SPSS version 21, with one factor explaining 71 % of the variance in items; all factor loadings > 0.7; Cronbach's $\alpha = 0.99$).
>
> However, we did not find good support for aggregating all items of the transactional leadership scale (average $r^*_{wg} = 0.41$; average $ICC1 = 0.07$ and $ICC2 = 0.25$). Items that measure non-contingent reward and punishment behaviors in particular showed very low levels of agreement, with contingent reward and punishment just below acceptable levels. Therefore, we decided to measure and analyze these behaviors at the individual level. Since contingent and non-contingent behavior and reward and punishment can be expected to

influence behavior in differing ways, we investigated the factor structure of these behaviors before aggregating the items to scales. An exploratory factor analysis with varimax rotation returned four factors, each a good representation of the four dimensions of contingent and non-contingent reward and punishment behavior. Only one item for contingent reward behavior was excluded because of a factor loading below 0.7 ("frequently does not acknowledge my good performance"). All four scales formed reliable and one-dimensional measures for the intended constructs (factor R^2 ranging from 15 to 21 %; all factor loadings > 0.73; Cronbach's $\alpha > 0.84$).

Much like many other measurement validation reports, this excerpt refers to commonly used thresholds at which the indices for agreement, reliability, and consistency were deemed acceptable. Although we did not find a "golden standard", there is an unspoken consensus of a sort among researchers for thresholds of 0.7 for r^*_{wg}, about 0.2 for ICC1, and about 0.4 for ICC2. This use of arbitrary thresholds as rules of thumb has been heavily criticized, and there is a rising call to use alternatives and include significance tests for some of these measures [13, 14]. Not surprisingly, as we discuss in Chap. 8, similar concerns have been raised about the use of significance tests. Therefore, the rules of thumb are to choose indices that seem most appropriate for the data and the particular study, to report all indices transparently, to investigate further when the indices are far from the accepted thresholds and explain why that may be the case, and to flank these statistical calculations with theoretical considerations. Finally, it is always a good idea to check recent literature to see whether any coefficient or threshold has been updated. (*Organizational Research Methods* is a journal that is worth keeping track of.) We elaborate further on some of these rules of thumb in Chap. 8.

Does the Data Require HLM?

HLM is required when studying nested data with variance at both the individual level and the group level. Therefore, HLM is *not* required when all variables vary at the same level of analysis—that is, when there is no clear grouping effect. In our example, HLM would not be required if every teacher's expectations for every student differed and if, on average, teachers didn't differ in what they expected of students—that is, they all think that certain students will do well and others won't, so there is no foreseeable difference between classes. Although our conceptual model and theoretical expectations reflect that we think teachers differ from each other and are consistent toward their students (leading to differences between classes), the data may tell us otherwise. In other words, in the unlikely event that (1) all measures of reliability, consistency and agreement indicate that variables should be analyzed at the individual level (as was the case for transactional leadership in our example) or (2) there is no difference between groups, we do not need HLM and can instead use normal regression or SEM. Therefore, the simple "between-group difference" is the first model that is typically run in HLM. It is unlikely to return insignificant results if all indicators of agreement, consistency, and reliability are up to standard. When these indicators are up to standard and the "between-group difference" (ANOVA) model is significant, we do need to run a HLM.

Understanding HLM

Returning to our example of students and their teachers, Fig. 5.1 illustrates our interest in how students' performance is affected by their IQ at the individual level (level 1) and by their teachers' expectations at the class level (level 2). We hypothesize that, at the student level, IQ (x) is positively related to performance (y). This simple effect, at the lowest level, could be estimated using the simple regression function:

$$\text{Level 1} \qquad Y_i = \beta_{0j} + \beta_{1j}X_{ij} + e_i$$

which is the same function we discussed at the beginning of Chap. 3, with one key difference: the j index. The j index represents the class students are in and, thus, the teacher they have. (If there were only one teacher, we would not need the j.) We also hypothesize that the teacher's expectation is positively related to her students' performance, an effect that we expect to manifest in a similar way for all the students in the same class but differently for all students of other classes. We could estimate a similar function as the one above (with x representing the teacher's expectations), but we would either lose individual-level variance or violate the assumption of independent errors. The solution provided by HLM is to estimate two second-level functions, one for each of the parameters of the level 1 function:

$$\text{Level 2} \qquad \beta_{0j} = \gamma_{00} + \gamma_{01}Z_j + r_{0j}$$

$$\beta_{1j} = \gamma_{10} + \gamma_{11}Z_j + r_{1j},$$

where z represents teachers' expectations. If we were to interpret these second-level models, we could say that the average student performance per class (β_{0j}) and the extent to which every IQ point relates to an increase in performance (β_{1j}) is a function of teacher expectations. This function, like the level 1 function, also has a to-be-estimated intercept (γ_{00}) and slope (γ_{11}) and an unknown error (r_{1j}). Figure 5.3 illustrates what level 1 equations may look like in different classes.

Figure 5.3 illustrates large level 1 differences in intercept (β_{0j}) and slope (β_{1j}) between two classes. The level 2 equations represent an attempt to estimate how much of and how that difference is influenced by the teachers' expectations (for all classes, not just two). The example suggests that the teachers' expectations affect

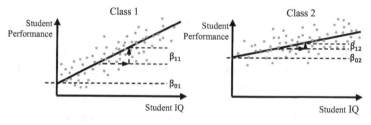

Fig. 5.3 Simplified illustration of the meaning of β_{0j} and β_{1j} in HLM

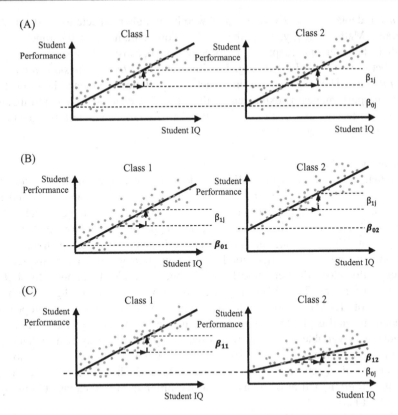

Fig. 5.4 Simplified illustration of possible effects of level 2 estimations on level 1 intercept (**b**), slope (**c**), and neither of both (**a**)

both the average student performance and the extent to which differences in performance are explained by IQ.

However, depending on whether our hypotheses hold, three other types of results are possible [1]. Figure 5.4a illustrates the (simplified) case in which teacher performance does not make a difference since *both intercept and slope parameters are similar* in every class. Therefore, mathematically, the level-2 slope parameters (γ_{01} and γ_{11}) will be 0, the level 1 slope and intercept will be affected only by the level 2 intercepts (γ_{00} and γ_{10}), and any small difference between groups is caused by the second-level error term (r_{1j}).

Figure 5.4b shows the case where teacher expectations do cause differences between groups in the intercept of the level 1 relationship. The example shown represents the scenario in which higher expectations lead to better performance, irrespective of the effect of IQ. This effect causes a shift in the *location* of the function relative to the y-axis (which is what the intercept β_{0j} represents), but no shift in the angle or slope (β_{1j}). This shift will translate into *an equal shift of the mean*: students in classes with teachers who have higher expectations do better on average. Mathematically, then, the level 2 slope parameter in the function that predicts the level 1 intercept (γ_{01}) is different from 0, causing the level 1 intercept to vary between groups. Finally, Fig. 5.4c illustrates an *effect on the slope but not on the intercept*, showing that varying teacher expectations influence how much of students' performance is explained by their IQs. For example, one could imagine that higher teacher expectations reduce the share of variance in performance that is explained by differences in IQ.

Executing HLM

Now that we understand how HLM works, we can talk about how to run the analysis. Different programs require different data structures and steps and use different notations and approaches. STATA and SAS refer to mixed models rather than HLM and express the second-level and higher-level equations as "variance components." This approach and notation is explained in Chap. 6, which introduces fixed-effect and random-effect models for longitudinal data. These models are conceptually close to hierarchical models but are typically applied to slightly different problems. The explanation we have provided is more aligned with the notation of HLM7,[1] an easy-to-use, stand-alone application developed by Raudenbush and Bryk [15] that is flexible in what it allows (e.g., latent variables, dichotomous variables). Garson ([3], Chap. 3) provides an extensive, hands-on introduction to running HLM using HLM7, including an overview of how to prepare two data sets (one at level 1, one at level 2), how to feed the data sets into the program, and how to ensure that the program "understands" the units of analysis at both levels.

The first step in any HLM or mixed model analysis is to run a full fixed-effects model, where no independent variables are introduced at level 1 or level 2. This kind of analysis is the equivalent of an ANOVA analysis that analyzes whether there is a difference between groups in the level 1 dependent variable. In HLM7, this analysis returns a "reliability estimate" and a "final estimation of variance component," which represent the ICC1 and the significance of the between-group variance, respectively. If the ICC1 is close to 0 or is negative, and the between-group variance is insignificant, you are unlikely to need to continue using HLM and can turn instead to other kinds of regression models (in this case they are likely to yield very similar results).

Next, independent variables can be introduced into both level 1 and level 2. A choice will have to be made concerning whether to introduce raw variable scores or to use either "group mean centering" or "grand mean centering." As the terms suggest, group mean centering subtracts the group mean from raw scores, and grand mean centering subtracts the mean for all individuals across all groups. Mean centering provides an intercept that is more easily interpretable than when using raw scores, as it represents the expected level of the dependent variable

---

[1] http://www.ssicentral.com/hlm/index.html

(performance, in our example) for a person with an average score on the independent variable (IQ). This average refers to either the average for their group (class) or the average for all individuals (students) [1]. The disadvantage of mean centering is that it can confound results, especially when the model contains multilevel mediation [16]. Zhang et al. [16] also explained an intuitive way of testing for mediation in multilevel models, although top journals often require the use of more robust methods (e.g., [17–19]).

Some researchers estimate each hypothesis separately by selectively introducing variables and then reporting results for each hypothesis test, while others introduce all variables at once. Either approach returns estimates for all intercept and slope parameters in the model, including *standard errors* and *t*-ratios, degrees of freedom, and *p*-values. The parameter estimates can be interpreted in the same way as those for regression and SEM (and as explained in the "Understanding HLM" section). The *t*-ratio and *p*-values can help you to evaluate whether the regression coefficients can be considered to differ sufficiently from 0 to be confident that there is an effect (see Chap. 8 for a discussion on the use of *p*-values).

Some programs offer results of estimates for both robust and non-robust standard errors. If these estimates differ markedly from each other, certain assumptions were probably violated, so you should correct for them (Chap. 8) and/or use the robust estimates. Whatever you decide to do, always transparently report all elements of the output and specify whether you reported the robust or non-robust standard errors, and why. The goal is for other researchers to be able to replicate your findings, so be transparent.

Finally, most programs will also allow you to calculate more advanced fit indices for your model, help you understand the explained variance in its components, plus much more. In fact, HLM is a much more versatile and complex method than we may have indicated in this chapter, the purpose of which was to provide first insights into what HLM is, when you should use it, and how. For more detailed information, consult Garson [3], Hofmann [1], or Chap. 5 of this book, which explains similar statistical struggles in a different way. Triangulation is key.

References

1. Hofmann DA (1997) An overview of the logic and rationale of hierarchical linear models. J Manage 23(6):723–744. doi:10.1177/014920639702300602
2. Hofmann DA, Griffin MA, Gavin MB (2000) The application of hierarchical linear modeling to organizational research. In: Klein KJ, Kozlowski SWJ (eds) Multi-level theory, research and methods in organizations: foundations, extensions, and new directions. Jossey-Bass, San Francisco, CA, pp 467–512
3. Garson GD (2013) Fundamentals of hierarchical linear and multilevel modeling. In: Garson GD (ed) Hierarchical linear modeling: guide and applications. Sage Publications, Thousand Oaks, CA, pp 3–25
4. Huta V (2014) When to use hierarchical linear modeling. Quant Methods Psychol 10(1):13–28
5. Peterson MF, Castro SL (2006) Measurement metrics at aggregate levels of analysis: implications for organization culture research and the GLOBE project. Leadersh Q 17(5):506–521. doi:10.1016/j.leaqua.2006.07.001

6. Lindell MK, Brandt CJ, Whitney DJ (1999) A revised index of interrater agreement for multi-item ratings of a single target. Appl Psychol Meas 23(2):127–135. doi:10.1177/01466219922031257

7. Bliese PD (2000) Within-group agreement, non-independence, and reliability: implications for data aggregation and analysis. In: Klein KJ, Kozlowski SWJ (eds) Multi-level theory, research and methods in organizations: foundations, extensions, and new directions. Jossey-Bass, San Francisco, CA, pp 349–381

8. Conway J, Huffcutt A (1997) Psychometric properties of multi-source performance ratings: a meta-analysis of subordinate, supervisor, peer, and self-ratings. Hum Perform 10:331–360

9. Lebreton JM, Burgess JRD, Kaiser RB, Atchley EK, James LR (2003) The restriction of variance hypothesis and interrater reliability and agreement: are ratings from multiple sources really dissimilar? Org Res Methods 6(1):80–128

10. Arnold JA, Arad S, Rhoades JA, Drasgow F (2000) The empowering leadership questionnaire: the construction and validation of a new scale for measuring leader behaviors. J Org Behav 21(3):249–269

11. Fong KH, Snape E (2014) Empowering leadership, psychological empowerment and employee outcomes: testing a multi-level mediating model. Br J Manage 126–138

12. Srivastava A, Bartol KM, Locke EA (2006) Empowering leadership in management teams: effects on knowledge sharing, efficacy, and performance. Acad Manage J 49(6):1239–1251

13. Cohen A, Doveh E, Nahum-Shani I (2009) Testing agreement for multi-item scales with the indices rWG(J) and ADM(J). Organ Res Methods 12(1):148–164

14. Dunlap WP, Burke MJ, Smith-Crowe K (2003) Accurate tests of statistical significance for r_{WG} and average deviation interrater agreement indexes. J Appl Psychol 88(2):356–362

15. Raudenbush SW, Bryk AS (2002) Hierarchical linear models: applications and data analysis methods. Sage Publications, Thousand Oaks, CA

16. Zhang Z, Zyphur MJ, Preacher KJ (2009) Testing multilevel mediation using hierarchical linear models: problems and solutions. Organ Res Methods 12:695–719. doi:10.1177/1094428108327450

17. Bauer DJ, Preacher KJ, Gil KM (2006) Conceptualizing and testing random indirect effects and moderated mediation in multilevel models: new procedures and recommendations. Psychol Methods 11:142–163

18. Preacher KJ, Hayes AF (2008) Asymptotic and resampling strategies for assessing and comparing indirect effects in multiple mediator models. Behav Res Methods 40:879–891

19. Preacher KJ, Zyphur MJ, Zhang Z (2010) A general multilevel SEM framework for assessing multilevel mediation. Psychol Methods 15:209–233

Analyzing Longitudinal and Panel Data

6

Data often comes from observations made at multiple points in time. Obtaining repeated observations on the same units allows the researcher to access a richer information set about observed units than would be possible with single observations and to map the evolution of the phenomenon over multiple periods for both individual units and overall as a trend. (For example, relationships between two variables may strengthen, weaken, or even disappear over time.) Longitudinal data can be gathered via survey instruments or archival databases that offer repeated measures on the same variables at different times.

Longitudinal data differ from cross-sectional data in two important ways: There are multiple observations for the same units, and there is a time dimension that can be exploited because the phenomenon is observed at different points in time. Therefore, data is nested across two dimensions: units and time. As a result, not all observations are independent of each other, thus violating one of the assumptions of multivariate data analysis. So, how do we deal with longitudinal data? What kind of tests and tools are available to exploit such richness?

This chapter examines the key features of longitudinal and panel data analysis by comparing it with the classic (OLS) regression models discussed in Chap. 3. The chapter provides guidance on data structures with multiple observations for the same units (N) at different points in time (T), on discerning between instances in which panel-data estimations are preferred over pooled-OLS estimations, on running fixed-effects or random-effects models, and on interpreting and reporting estimations from these models. Because these topics are complex, we discuss the choice of the appropriate method toward the end of the chapter.

6.1   What Are Longitudinal and Panel Data?

Many research questions require us to obtain and analyze data on the observed units at multiple points in time. Consider, for example, the question concerning whether firms' investments in research and development (R&D) affect profitability. If we

© Springer International Publishing Switzerland 2017
W. Mertens et al., *Quantitative Data Analysis*, DOI 10.1007/978-3-319-42700-3_6

simplify reality a bit, we can assume that firms plan the next year's investment based on past endeavors and forecasts about future prospects, threats, and opportunities. Finding the answer to questions like whether firms' investments in R&D affect profitability differs from testing hypotheses across *levels* of treatment at *one point in time*, as instead of *levels*, we are interested in analyzing the *changes over time* that units undergo. Analyzing such longitudinal phenomena involves dealing with data structures that differ from cross-sectional data [1].

The most important difference between longitudinal data and cross-sectional data is that longitudinal data adds a *time* dimension such that variables change across units (N) *and* time (T). As a result, researchers have data on individual units (n_i) observed across multiple dimensions at various points in time. In other words, units differ across individuals (a "between-variation") at the same point in time but also internally across time (a "within-variation").

Gathering Longitudinal Data

Gathering longitudinal data is often complex and expensive because it entails obtaining information on the same variables in at least two *waves*. One example of a successful longitudinal study is the Household, Income and Labour Dynamics (HILDA) in Australia, which has is funded by the Commonwealth's government and made public to researchers and institutions.[1]

Panel data structures are a particular type of longitudinal data, where one can collect information about the *same variables and individuals* at several points in time [2]. Broadly speaking, panel data are of two types:

- *Balanced panel data*: All observed units *i* have data across all waves *(t)*. For example, if you survey 100 individuals (N = 100) at five points in time (T = 5), balanced panel data will have 500 observations (i.e., N × T). Balanced panel data are often difficult to obtain because of the challenge in retaining participants over time (e.g., *survivorship bias*).
- *Unbalanced panel data*: These are the most diffuse form of longitudinal data, as researchers do not have data about the same units in each wave. For example, the HILDA survey is currently on its fourteenth wave (hence, T = 14) and covers an average of 19,000 individuals (N = 19,000) in each wave. A few individuals have been surveyed in all waves, but the majority has been included in five or six, and some have been included only once. Therefore, HILDA is an example of longitudinal unbalanced panel data.

One of the strengths of longitudinal data (particularly balanced panel data) is its potential for supporting causal relationships because of its ability to deal with observable and unobservable effects better than cross-sectional data can. However,

---

[1]The household, income and labour dynamics in Australia (Hilda) survey is maintained by the Melbourne institute and all editions and addenda are available at https://www.melbourneinstitute.com/hilda/

if the units included in the sample vary from wave to wave (i.e., the data are unbalanced), then the longitudinal data will resemble a set of cross-sectional data sets measured at multiple points in time, and the benefits of having longitudinal data will be reduced because only the time dimension, not the within-unit variation in time, can be exploited. One type of longitudinal data is *time series* data, which are characterized by a relatively small number of units (N) observed at multiple points in time (T): In such cases, T is much larger than N. In spite of their popularity and applications in financial economics and monetary policy,[2] time series data have not gained popularity in accounting and information systems research.

Several key decisions must be made when deciding how to collect longitudinal data for analysis, one of which concerns the *time interval*: how often or at what distance in time should data be gathered? While this decision may be relatively easy in archival financial accounting research, as financial statements are released every quarter, it is not so simple in other settings. Some things to bear in mind when defining the time interval, especially when employing surveys, include:

- *Attrition*: Units that have been included in one wave of data collection may not respond to or be available for subsequent waves. This problem is particularly tricky if patterns of non-respondents emerge, creating a selection bias. Sample size can shrink as a result of attrition.
- *Length of Interval*: The difference in time between waves can affect whether changes are allowed to unfold; short intervals may not allow for sufficient changes, whereas long intervals may introduce confounding factors that require more data to be collected.
- *Stratification:* If a number of units or individuals drop out from one wave to the next, new respondents must be selected to be part of the pool and replace observed units that have dropped out. These replacements are necessary to ensure the population remains sufficiently large to be representative.

Understanding Longitudinal Data and Its Variance
A key feature of longitudinal data structures is that the total variance of observed variables can be split into *within*-variation and *between*-variation. Within-variation refers to the variability induced by observing the same unit i at several points in time. For example, individuals' income levels may change from year to year (Fig. 6.1). Between-individual variation relates to variability between subjects at a single point in time. This variation is intuitive since cross-sectional data already offer a degree of between-individual variation.

Figure 6.1 shows graphically a longitudinal data structure that contains data about annual income (income_id) for three individuals (N = 3) at five points in time (T = 5), so there are 15 individual-year observations nested within individuals

---

[2]Two examples of where the N is small compared to the data points are studies about changes in exchange rates (one currency over multiple quarters) and high-frequency data on stock prices (where observations come down to minutes or seconds).

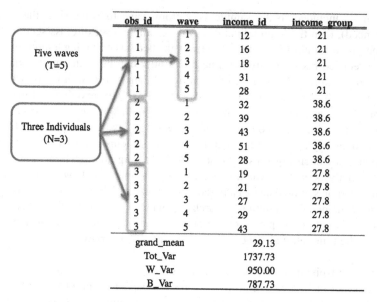

obs_id	wave	income_id	income_group
1	1	12	21
1	2	16	21
1	3	18	21
1	4	31	21
1	5	28	21
2	1	32	38.6
2	2	39	38.6
2	3	43	38.6
2	4	51	38.6
2	5	28	38.6
3	1	19	27.8
3	2	21	27.8
3	3	27	27.8
3	4	29	27.8
3	5	43	27.8
grand_mean		29.13	
Tot_Var		1737.73	
W_Var		950.00	
B_Var		787.73	

Five waves (T=5)

Three Individuals (N=3)

Fig. 6.1 Example of a longitudinal data structure

(obs_id) and years (wave). The average income across all observations (i.e., the grand mean) is 29.13. Average income for each individual (income_group) is reported for all three individual (21, 38.6, and 27.8, respectively).

Figure 6.1 also summarizes three aspects of the variance in the data of *income_id*: *total*, *within-individual*, and *between-individual* variance. These parts of the variance are usually referred to as Sums of Squares (SS) because of how they are computed:

$$\text{Within-Individual Variance} \quad = \Sigma_i\Sigma_t \left(Y_{it} - \overline{Y}_i\right)^2 \quad = 950.00$$
$$\text{Between-Individual Variance} \quad = \Sigma_i\Sigma_t \left(\overline{Y}_i - \overline{Y}\right)^2 \quad = 787.73$$
$$\text{Total Variance} \quad = \Sigma_i\Sigma_t \left(Y_{it} - \overline{Y}\right)^2 \quad = 1737.73$$

In other words, the variance components consist of the distance of individual scores (in each wave) from individual means (within-variance), the distance of individual means from the total mean (between-variance), and the average distance of individual scores from the total mean (total variance). The three individuals differ, one earning more than the others, and between-individual variation is large (45 % of the total variance). Individuals also differ internally because of the large variation in their income at different times. As a consequence, within-individual variance also accounts for a large portion of total variance (55 % of the total variance). Variance decomposition is the first step in assessing whether the data present patterns and can be clustered. In this case, individual-level effects should be taken into account.

6.2 Clustering as a Way to Deal with Nestedness

Another way of looking at longitudinal data is by focusing on the interpretation of estimation coefficients, standard errors, and t-statistics. A number of issues should be taken into account when the preferred estimation strategy is OLS, as in the pooled-OLS approach, *clustering* of observations can result in biased estimates. The main feature of longitudinal data is that the dependent variable (outcome, Y) and the independent variables (treatment, X) can be correlated along a series of dimensions known as *clusters*. The most frequent types of clusters are time-series correlation and cross-sectional correlation.

Time-series (or serial) correlation occurs when the same units (e.g., individuals, groups, firms) are correlated over time, so observations for firm i at time t are linked with those for firm i at time $t-1$ or $t+1$. Such correlations make intuitive sense as, for example, corporations' net income and governance variables tend to be sticky and do not change much over time, so they are likely to be correlated at two consecutive points in time. Likewise, individual-level attributes like talent, education, and income have limited variability over time, especially when the observation window is not large and t is not too distant from $t-1$. When observed values do not change much over time, the individual-level *homogeneity* leads to clustering issues within units. The time-series dependency is rarely accounted for in OLS estimations.

Cross-sectional correlation, which is more intuitive and diffuse than time-series correlation, occurs when units are correlated at the same point in time, such as when firm i at time t is correlated with firm k at time t. This form of correlation can be explained by temporal effects on economic or financial variables (e.g., stock prices) or levels of technological development that change over time and affect all units in the cross-section.

Failing to account for such clustering results in biased estimation coefficients, systematic underestimation of standard errors, and overestimation of t-statistics [2,3], and the likelihood of rejecting the null-hypothesis (of no effect) when it is actually true increases markedly. Petersen [4] offered a thorough examination of these issues through a simulation of the extent of the bias caused by failure to account for either or both types of clustering effects in OLS estimations [4].

Table 6.1 offers a visual representation of clustering of N individuals over T time periods in a panel-data setting. The variables included are stock returns (*ret*) during the observation period, leverage (*lev*) at the end of each period t, and audit fees (*fees*) in each period.

Table 6.1 reports identical data using two forms of clustering: by time and by unit. *Panel A* shows the effects of *cross-sectional dependency*, where time is the clustering variable. Cross-sectional dependence is relevant for some variables, but not all. For example, the variable for reporting stock returns for firm i at time t seems to have a strong time effect. Stock market returns are affected by an overall macro-economic scenario and changes in monetary policy, so we would expect that returns for each firm are correlated cross-sectionally in any given year. This is evident in Panel A, where the average returns for the N observation in each year

Table 6.1 Effects of clustering

Panel A: Clustering by time

Obs_id	Year	Ret	Ret_yr_avg	Lev	Lev_yr_avg	Fees	Fees_yr_avg
1001	1	−2.50	**−3.60**	0.30	**0.35**	120	**161.25**
1002	1	2.00	**−3.60**	0.15	**0.35**	65	**161.25**
1003	1	−5.90	**−3.60**	0.38	**0.35**	160	**161.25**
100 N	1	−8.00	**−3.60**	0.55	**0.35**	300	**161.25**
1001	2	3.00	8.25	0.32	0.34	108	139.50
1002	2	4.00	8.25	0.10	0.34	60	139.50
1003	2	13.00	8.25	0.40	0.34	140	139.50
100 N	2	13.00	8.25	0.55	0.34	250	139.50
1001	3	12.00	**10.50**	0.31	**0.33**	116	**178.00**
1002	3	8.00	**10.50**	0.13	**0.33**	64	**178.00**
1003	3	6.00	**10.50**	0.35	**0.33**	152	**178.00**
100 N	3	16.00	**10.50**	0.52	**0.33**	380	**178.00**
1001	T	15.00	14.25	0.30	0.33	124	170.00
1002	T	14.00	14.25	0.14	0.33	70	170.00
1003	T	16.00	14.25	0.36	0.33	166	170.00
100 N	T	12.00	14.25	0.50	0.33	320	170.00

Panel B: Clustering by unit

Obs_id	Year	Ret	Ret_id_avg	Lev	Lev_id_avg	Fees	Fees_id_avg
1001	1	−2.50	6.88	0.30	0.31	120	117
1001	2	3.00	6.88	0.32	0.31	108	117
1001	3	12.00	6.88	0.31	0.31	116	117
1001	T	15.00	6.88	0.30	0.31	124	117
1002	1	2.00	**7.00**	0.15	**0.13**	65	**64.75**
1002	2	4.00	**7.00**	0.10	**0.13**	60	**64.75**
1002	3	8.00	**7.00**	0.13	**0.13**	64	**64.75**
1002	T	14.00	**7.00**	0.14	**0.13**	70	**64.75**
1003	1	−5.90	7.28	0.38	0.37	160	154.50
1003	2	13.00	7.28	0.40	0.37	140	154.50
1003	3	6.00	7.28	0.35	0.37	152	154.50
1003	T	16.00	7.28	0.36	0.37	166	154.50
100 N	1	−8.00	**8.25**	0.55	**0.53**	300	**287.50**
100 N	2	13.00	**8.25**	0.55	**0.53**	250	**287.50**
100 N	3	16.00	**8.25**	0.52	**0.53**	280	**287.50**
100 N	T	12.00	**8.25**	0.50	**0.53**	320	**287.50**

Obs_id is the identifier for each unit observed; **year** indicates the time (year) when the observation was made; **Ret** is the yearly buy-hold return for a given stock; **ret_id_avg** expresses the average return for each unit across the different times; **Lev** is the firm's leverage in a given year whereas **lev_id_avg** is the firm's average value of leverage during the observation period. **Fees** is the total amount of audit fees paid to the external auditor; **fees_id_avg** indicates the average value of fees paid by a firm in the observation period changes markedly across time. Specifically, in year 1 the variable for reporting stock returns seems to be negative compared to years 2 and 3. The last year of observation (T) has the strongest and more positive returns of all.

Table 6.1 reports no time effect for the "leverage" variable, as the average value is stable over time (around 0.34). This result should be expected since firms do not change their capital structure often. Last, the variable for audit fees shows a significant time-clustering effect, which should also be expected since average audit fees can change over time as a result of regulatory changes, litigation threats, or increased risk in the audit market. As a result, time-clustering occurs because the average value for the N observations change significantly over the 4 years the data covers.

Table 6.1's *Panel B* reveals potential *time-series clustering*. Given that the same individuals are observed over multiple times, it is likely that observations will be serially correlated. Contrary to the result in Panel A, the variable for returns does not show individual-level clustering, as returns are affected by market-wide and time effects. This result should be expected given that stock returns (unlike stock price or earnings) are random, so they should not be related to the previous year's or the next year's returns. (Otherwise, information would be plugged into price earlier on.) The N observations are close in terms of average returns, and there is limited firm-level effect, so time clustering is should be considered more in relation to the variable for returns. The results for leverage in Panel B differ from those in Panel A. *Leverage* is a highly stationary variable; it does not have a *cross-sectional correlation* but a strong *time-series correlation* because firms choose their capital structures and leverage amount and tend to stick to them over time. Units are internally homogeneous over the T periods, whereas they differ markedly between each other. In the case of *leverage*, time-series dependency is greater than *cross-sectional correlation*.

Last, the variable for *audit fees* shows a certain degree of *time-series* correlation since firms tend to be internally homogeneous across years. However, the firms tend to be within a range of *fees* that changes between firms and with time. *Fees* is a likely candidate to suffer both *time-series* and *cross-sectional dependencies*.

Tools and Remedies to Control for Both Types of Dependencies The literature offers numerous tools, known as *clustering procedures*, to deal with correlations in observations originating from panel data [1, 5, 6] and rule out concerns that are due to potential double-clustering issues:

- *OLS regression with white standard errors (Rogers)*: One of OLS's assumptions is that the observations are uncorrelated and the error term is randomly distributed. In longitudinal data, observations are clustered along a *time* dimension and/or *individual* dimension. In other words, OLS is not suited to making correct inferences in longitudinal data and will produce mis-specified test statistics when either form of correlation is present. The White [7] standard errors correction [7], which is common in accounting studies, can address the heteroscedasticity issue—that is, the size or value of observed variables differs between units—but not the *time* or *cross-sectional dependence* in the data[3];

- *Fama-MacBeth cross-sectional estimation:* Fama and MacBeth [8] designed a tool to address concerns about cross-sectional correlation [8]. In finance, time exerts a strong effect on market prices, volatility, and risk. Fama-MacBeth's cross-sectional estimation (FMB-cs) results in a series of separate estimations for each period. In essence, FMB-cs runs T separate regressions for each period t, and the estimation coefficients and standard errors are weighted and averaged to come up with a unique point estimate. FMB-cs estimations return consistent and unbiased estimates when there is no *time-series correlation* (i.e., individual units are not correlated over time), but they are not appropriate when both types of dependencies are present. In relation to the example in Table 6.1, the *returns* variable showed a cross-sectional correlation, but not a time-series correlation.

- *Fama-MacBeth time-series estimation:* The Fama-MacBeth time-series estimation is a revision of the FMB-cs estimation process. Clustering is not on the time dimension but at the unit level (FMB-ts), and the source of dependency comes from within individuals. The estimation procedure is the same as that in FMB-cs, but clustering changes through an estimation of N different regressions (one per individual) and then the estimation coefficients and standard errors are averaged. This revision of the original FMB-cs estimation is appropriate when there is *time-series* correlation but time does not exert any influence on the variables. In Table 6.1, the variable *leverage* showed consistency over time but no clear patterns in yearly data. FMB-ts does not correct for both time and individual clustering, so in the presence of both, it yields inconsistent estimates.[4]

- *Newey-West estimation:* the Newey-West estimation [9] is a refinement of the White [7] standard errors because Newey-West takes into account the *time-series correlation*—for example, individual observations are correlated over time—but assumes *cross-sectional* independence [9]. While Newey-West returns consistent estimates in the presence of serial dependence, it performs poorly when time exerts an effect on the variables. Both Petersen's [4] simulation and Gow, Ormazabal, and Taylor's review [2] discuss the limitations of the Newey-West approach in the presence of both sources of dependencies [2].[5]

- *One-way clustering:* One-way clustering considers only one level of clustering in the data. It allows clustering along one dimension (either time or individual), so if one cannot rule out a second potential source of dependencies, an

---

[3]The STATA routine to estimate OLS with White-robust standard errors is *regress y x, robust.*

[4]The command to perform Fama-MacBeth [8] estimation is similar for both the FMB-cs and FMB-ts types of regressions. Mitchell Petersen of Northwestern University posts the codes for a series of popular software with which the FMB estimation can be performed at http://www.kellogg.northwestern.edu/faculty/petersen/htm/papers/se/se_programming.htm

[5]We refer readers to Petersen's webpage (please check footnote 7 in Petersen's webpage), which provides codes for the Newey-West routine.

estimation will yield biased results that overestimate the rejection rate of the null-hypothesis.[6]

- *Two-way clustering:* Two-way clustering is warranted when both *time-series* and *cross-sectional dependencies* are present in the data. One example in Table 6.1 is the variable *fees*, where the level of audit fees changes at both an individual firm-level and between years. While two-way clustering is superior to all of the estimation approaches seen before, it can reduce variation in the variables, thus losing some valuable information [3,4]. For instance, when the number of clusters is small, it can lead to issues in estimating the standard errors.[7]

The choice of clustering should not be made ex-ante. All approaches have advantages and downsides, and careful consideration and a thorough variance decomposition analysis will suggest what is at stake and what one is trading off. As so often occurs in empirical work, we should examine all analyses, compare the findings, and choose the most suitable strategy to report. There are two important caveats: first, the number of *clusters* can exceed two when industry or location is taken into account. (This chapter does not cover these issues, but there are great books and resources that can help! [6]) Second, one way to control for *cross-sectional* (time) and *time-series* (individual) clustering is to employ indicator variables for years and one-way clustering for individuals. This approach is especially suitable when T is small.

6.3   Which Models Can We Use to Analyze Longitudinal Data?

Now that we understand the differences between longitudinal and cross-sectional data, we turn to how these differences affect the analysis of such data. Exploiting the features of longitudinal data can be helpful in overcoming some of the issues related to ensuring that changes in X causes changes in Y. (See Chap. 7 for a more in-depth overview of endogeneity and causality issues.) Longitudinal data are useful in capitalizing changes in status that occur at an individual level in order to offer a cleaner setting in which to claim causality. Longitudinal data offer the opportunity to use a broad range of estimation models that should be carefully evaluated in order to select the most appropriate approach This section compares three models: the pooled-OLS model, the fixed-effects model, and the random-effects model.

---

[6]The routine in STATA to perform one-way clustering is simple: either (1) *regress y x, cluster (id)* if *time-series correlation* is a concern, or (2) *regress y x, cluster (time)* if *cross-sectional correlation* is the main problem.

[7]Petersen's website offers a great deal of help in the estimation of OLS with two-way clustering. The routine is simple: cluster2 *y x,* fcluster(*id*) tcluster(*time*).

In the context of longitudinal data, a typical regression model is the **pooled-OLS regression**, which can be employed if observations are independent. In essence, *pooling* means treating all individual-year (or any combination of unit and time) data as unique and independent observations, so one can resort to normal OLS estimation[8] as in a cross-sectional analysis. Hence, a researcher does not establish that observations are clustered at an individual level. For example, if we had repeated observations (five waves at different points in time) for 100 individuals, pooled-OLS regression views these as 500 independent observations, which it uses to estimate regression coefficients. Thus, the pooled OLS does not recognize potential *within-individual variation*, and it treats all variability as *between-variation* (much as in a cross-sectional analysis). In other words, pooled OLS ignores the fact that observations are nested within individuals and assumes independence of observations. This assumption will likely result in inflated sample sizes, biased coefficients, and underestimation of standard errors. Because of these biases, panel data usually calls for the use of more appropriate models, the two most common of which are fixed-effects models and random effects models.

Fixed-Effects (FE) Models

FE models are preferable to OLS models for analyzing longitudinal data because FE models allow the researcher to control for unobservable *time-invariant* factors, that is, factors that do not change over time. Some individual and organizational traits, such as a person's gender and ethnicity, are time-invariant by definition. Other traits could vary over time but often do not change during the study, such as the location of an organization's headquarters and the political climate. Even though these factors do not change over time, they diff for every unit of analysis. Individuals in our study can have different genders, and different organizations can have different locations. In "normal" OLS regression models, these individual factors are typically captured in the error term, but OLS models assume that these error terms are independent. This assumption is violated if observations are taken from the same individual: gender at time 1 for person 1 will be the same as the gender of that same person at time 2 (barring highly exceptional cases). FE models do not assume this independence of errors *within* the same units across time, which is why they lead to accurate estimations of effects in longitudinal data.

FE models are particularly useful when researchers do not have access to data that captures these time-invariant variables. There are many elements of the people, organizations, and context in which they operate (e.g., political climate, regulations, reporting standards, personality) that are hard to capture in simple variables or that are outside the scope of the study. However, these contextual or personal variables can still influence the study. We discuss the problems related to

---

[8]To be consistent with a large body of literature in accounting and finance [3,4], we use the expression "pooled-OLS regression" but refer to all types of regression approaches (e.g., logit or probit, which are commonly used) wherein the regression model specified does not take into account the fact that the data have a longitudinal structure.

these omitted correlated variables in detail in Chap. 7; for now, just recognize that FE models allow researchers to control for these unmeasured influencing variables.

Notwithstanding the important advantage of working well when researchers do not have access to data that captures time-invariant variables, FE models do not model the *effect* of time-invariant variables and FE-models do not control for unobserved variables that *do* change over time. Random-effects (RE) models solve at least part of this problem.

Random-Effects (RE) Models

RE models differ from FE models in their use of *time-invariant variables* in estimations. The RE model makes more efficient use of the data than the FE model does because the RE model exploits both the within-unit and between-unit variability by weighting the relevance of the two sources of variability and partitioning it, whereas FE models exploit only the within-unit variability. In the extreme case, when the variability is entirely due to within-unit variation, RE estimation is identical to FE estimation.

The key features of RE models are that they provide efficient estimations of model parameters by using both between-unit and within-unit variance, allow for the impact of time-invariant variables on Y (differently from FE), and provide reliable estimates of the individual effects.

The use of RE models depends on the amount of unobservable time-invariant factors that are left out of the estimation. If there are too many, then FE models are more likely to provide unbiased estimates. Of course, the method and the diagnostic tool cannot be substitutes for thorough assessment and knowledge of the underlying data structure. The products of diagnostic tools, like p-values, should be interpreted as indications, not as definitive answers to the research design issue we face in answering research questions.

Notation

The importance of the time component also makes the notation of the models used to analyze panel data important. The equation model is specified as:

Panel data notation:

$$Y_{it} = \alpha_0 + \beta_1 X_{it}^1 + \beta_n X_i^n + v_{it} \tag{6.1}$$

where Y_{it} is the value of the outcome variable for unit i at time t, X_{it}^1 expresses the value of the main predictor (X^1) for unit i at time t, X_i^n is a covariate that takes the same value for each individual i, and the error tem v_{it} has two components—ε_{it} is specific to the unit-time, so it changes across individuals and time, and μ_i is specific to the units and does not change over time. Both Y_{it} and X_{it} are *time-variant variables:* they vary for the same unit over time. (For example, income and education are likely to change over time.) X_i^n is also *time-invariant.* (For example, the year of birth or ethnicity does not change for individuals, and the year of foundation or the State of first incorporation does not vary for firms). Distinguishing between time-variant and time-invariant variables is important in understanding longitudinal data.

6.4 Estimating and Reporting Fixed-Effects and Random-Effects Models

This section explains how to estimate fixed-effects and random-effects models by comparing the models with each other and with OLS to clarify the differences. The research question we use to illustrate these models concerns whether *R&D expenses enhance a company's market value*.

Step 1: Understanding Your Data

We discussed the specifics of longitudinal data in Sect. 6.1; here we illustrate what the data looks like for our example. Table 6.2 reports the structure of some data that can be summarized as follows:

$N = 20$ individual firms (units).
$T = 5$ years, so data are collected over 5 years at 1-year intervals.
$N \times T = 100$ firm-year observations.

Table 6.2 Snapshot of data on R&D expenses and market capitalization

Obs_id	Year	Ipo_year	Mtk_cap	Rd_exp_chg	Bod_size	Founder
10001	1	1980	260	4	18	1
10001	2	1980	280	4.8	18	1
10001	3	1980	248	−2	15	0
10001	4	1980	256	3	15	0
10001	5	1980	254	−0.5	15	0
10002	1	1983	280	1.9	17	1
10002	2	1983	276	2.1	17	1
10002	3	1983	268	1.1	15	0
10002	4	1983	270	2.2	15	0
10002	5	1983	274	2	15	0
...	...	...	...	...	...	...
10020	1	2015	12	1	3	0
10020	2	2015	16	3.2	5	1
10020	3	2015	14	−3	5	1
10020	4	2015	18	2.5	5	1
10020	5	2015	11	1.8	5	0

Obs_id is the identifier for each unit observed; **year** indicates the time (year) when the observation was made; **mkt_cap** is the total market value of firm i at the end of the fiscal year t. **rd_exp_chg** expresses the percentage change in R&D expenses from the previous year (t−1) to the current year (t0); **ipo_year** indicates the year in which the company went public; **bod_size** is the number of directors on the board at the end of the fiscal year; **founder** is a dummy variable that takes the value of 1 if the founder still holds an executive position in the firm, and 0 otherwise

There are five variables employed in the example:

- *Market Capitalization (mkt_cap)* indicates the total market value of firm *i* at the end of the fiscal year *t*. It is a time-variant dependent variable, given the research question of interest (Y_{it}).
- *R&D expenses (rd_exp_chg)* expresses the percentage change in R&D expenses from the previous year (t_{-1}) to the current year (t_0) for each firm *i*. It is a time-variant variable and the main predictor in the analysis (X_{it}).
- *Year of IPO (ipo_year)* indicates the year in which the company went public. This is a time-invariant variable because it is stable for each firm *i* over the 5 years of data. The extant literature suggests employing *ipo_year* as a control variable because it can affect market value (Y) and the R&D expense policy for firm *i* (X);
- *Board size (bod_size)* is the number of directors on the board at the end of the fiscal year. This is a time-variant variable, as it changes across firms and for each firm across time. Prior evidence suggests that larger boards are associated with larger market capitalization (Y) and a higher level of R&D expenses (X). Failing to include this variable leads to an omitted correlated variable problem (Chap. 7).
- *Active founder (founder)* is a dummy variable that takes the value of 1 if the founder still holds an executive position in the firm, and 0 otherwise. *Founder* is a time-variant variable, as founders may drop out of and re-join the firm in any of the 5 years of observation.

Table 6.3 reports the summary statistics for the variables in the sample.

The main features of the data should be well understood before undertaking more complex statistical analyses. Longitudinal data differ from cross-sectional data because of the time dimension (T); Table 6.4 re-displays the data aggregated by year.

Table 6.3 Summary statistics

Variable	Obs	Mean	Std. dev.	Min	Max
mtk_cap	100	164.85	82.59	11	280
rd_exp_chg	100	1.81	1.54	−3.0	4.8
ipo_year	100	2001	10.60	1980	2015
bod_size	100	9.18	4.17	1	18
founder	100	0.50	0.50	0	1

Table 6.4 Exploring the time dimension of data

Year	Mtk_cap		Rd_exp_chg		Bod_size		Founder	
	Mean	Sd	Mean	Sd	Mean	Sd	Mean	Sd
1	165.75	85.87	1.89	1.16	9.15	4.77	0.55	0.51
2	168.00	87.46	2.35	0.91	9.15	4.63	0.55	0.51
3	164.75	80.62	1.79	2.00	9.30	4.31	0.50	0.51
4	165.40	83.46	1.69	1.74	9.25	3.88	0.50	0.51
5	160.35	83.81	1.36	1.60	9.05	3.61	0.40	0.50

A close inspection of Table 6.4 reveals changes over time across *market capitalization*, *R&D expenses*, and the *founder's* involvement into executive positions. These changes indicate that time affects both Y (*mkt_cap*) and X (*rd_exp_chg*): specifically, market capitalization and R&D expenses decline over time, suggesting that macroeconomics conditions affect firms' and markets' behaviors. The variable *ipo_year* is not reported because it does not change over time.

Step 2: Variance Decomposition

The next step is a ***variance decomposition analysis*** in order to ascertain whether the variability of the outcome (*mkt_cap*) is due to firm-level changes over time (*within_var*) or to differences across firms (*btw_var*). The grand mean of *mkt_cap* is 164.85 (Table 6.3), but the individual means of each observation ($\overline{Y}_i$) range from 14.2 to 273.6.

The summary results for variance decomposition are as follows:

Total variance (market capitalization) = 675,346
Within-unit variance (market capitalization) = 6112
Between-unit variance (market capitalization) = 669,234

The results indicate that *mkt_cap* changes more between individuals than it does for individual firms during the observation window. The *F*-statistic for between-individual variation is high and significant (461.43; $p < 0.001$), suggesting that individuals are internally highly homogeneous—the intra-class correlation coefficient is 0.99, so nestedness must be taken into account—and firms vary significantly from one another.

Before moving to an analysis in a multivariate framework, we inspect the correlation matrix to uncover existing relationships among the data (Table 6.5).

Table 6.5 reveals patterns in the data that include a positive and significant relationship between *mkt_cap* and *rd_exp_chg* (0.28; $p < 0.01$), suggesting that changes in the level of R&D and market capitalization are positively associated. *bod_size* positively correlates with both market capitalization (0.88; $p < 0.001$) and R&D (0.23; $p < 0.05$), so *bod_size* must be included as a covariate in the OLS or panel data estimations. Similarly, *founder* is correlated with *mtk_cap* (-0.20; $p < 0.05$) and only marginally with *rd_exp_chg* (0.16; $p > 0.1$). *IPO_year* negatively correlates with both *mkt_cap* (-0.89; $p < 0.01$) and *rd_exp_chg* (-0.16; $p < 0.1$), suggesting the possibility of including it as a covariate in the regression model. Finally, *year* does not show significant correlations with any of the other variables, with a partial exception of *rd_epx_chg*.

Step 3: Estimation of the Model, Option 1: Pooled OLS

Now moving to data analysis, consider that we used a "normal" **pooled-OLS regression** to evaluate the relationship between the main predictor (*rd_exp_chg*) and the outcome of interest (*mkt_cap*) by taking into account a series of covariates

Table 6.5 Correlation matrix

	Mtk_cap	Rd_exp_chg	Bod_size	Founder	Ipo_year
rd_exp_chg	*0.28*				
	0.01				
bod_size	*0.88*	*0.23*			
	0.00	0.02			
founder	*−0.20*	0.16	*−0.25*		
	0.05	0.11	0.01		
ipo_year	*−0.89*	−0.16	*−0.90*	*0.31*	
	0.00	0.10	0.00	0.00	
year	−0.02	−0.16	0.00	−0.10	0.00
	0.82	0.12	0.97	0.33	1.00

Values in italics indicate a significant coefficient at a 5 % level. **Mkt_cap** is the total market value of firm i at the end of the fiscal year t. **rd_exp_chg** expresses the percentage change in R&D expenses from the previous year (t−1) to the current year (t0); **ipo_year** indicates the year in which the company went public; **bod_size** is the number of directors on the board at the end of the fiscal year; **founder** is a dummy variable that takes the value of 1 if the founder still holds an executive position in the firm, and 0 otherwise

(or control variables) that help to improve estimation efficiency or reduce the extent of a bias that may be due to omitted correlated variables (Chap. 7). Prior literature has suggested that two additional variables are jointly correlated with market capitalization and R&D expenses: *CEO compensation* and *Tax incentives*. These two variables cannot be included in the analysis because of data unavailability, so an omitted correlated variable (OCV) problem and biased estimations are triggered. *CEO compensation* is time-variant (i.e., firms change CEO compensation at varying times), whereas *Tax incentives* is time-invariant in the observed period (i.e., firms either obtain or do not obtain tax incentives). This distinction is relevant insofar as the panel data estimation (by both FE models and RE models) can deal with time-invariant heterogeneity, while OLS regression cannot do much. (Because of unobservable factors, neither panel-data nor OLS can deal with unobserved time-variant heterogeneity [10].) Pooled OLS regression does not take into account the fact that observed firms (N = 20) are not independent but are repeatedly observed at various points in time (T = 5).

For the sake of completeness and ease of comparison with panel-data estimation, we present two OLS models: OLS_short, which includes only two time-variant covariates (*ipo_year* and *bod_size*) and excludes *founder* (time invariant), and OLS_long, which includes all three covariates.

OLS_short:

$$Mkt\_cap_i = \alpha_0 + \beta_1 rd\_exp\_chg_i + \beta_2 founder_i + \beta_3 bod\_size_i + \varepsilon_i \qquad (6.2)$$

OLS_long:

Table 6.6 Comparison of pooled-OLS estimations

DV: *mkt_cap*	Model OLS_short		Model OLS_long	
	Coeff (se)	T	Coeff (se)	t
rd_exp_chg	4.16 (2.78)	1.50	5.07 (2.36)	2.15
bod_size	16.96 (1.04)	16.32	6.41 (1.93)	3.33
founder	0.28 (8.50)	0.03	9.20 (7.37)	1.25
ipo_year			−4.69 (0.76)	−6.16
intercept	1.45 (11.71)	0.12	9483 (1539)	6.16
Adj-R^2	0.77		0.83	
F-test	107.02 ($p < 0.001$)		121 ($p < 0.001$)	

$$Mkt\_cap_i = \alpha_0 + \beta_1 rd\_exp\_chg_i + \beta_2 founder_i + \beta_3 bod\_size_i$$
$$+ \beta_4 ipo\_year_i + \varepsilon_i \qquad (6.3)$$

Table 6.6's results differ depending on the specified model. Both OLS_short and OLS_long have high adjusted-R^2 (0.77 and 0.83, respectively), highlighting the two models' significant predictive ability. Despite their predictive ability, the two estimations differ along a number of dimensions:

- The coefficient on the main predictor *rd_exp_chg* is non-significant in OLS_short (4.16; $p > 0.10$), whereas it becomes larger and statistically significant in OLS_long (5.07, $p < 0.05$). This shift in OLS_long would prompt a rejection of the null hypothesis)and indicate support for the theoretical prediction.
- The coefficient on *bod_size* changes its magnitude and significance level. Although remaining large and strongly positive, in model OLS_long the size of the effect becomes nearly a third of the effect shown in OLS_short.
- The coefficient on *founder* becomes large (yet not statistically significant) in OLS_long, whereas it is close to zero in OLS_short.
- The *intercept* becomes a meaningful predictor of *market capitalization* in OLS_long (9483; $p < 0.001$), while it is not significant in OLS_short.

What drives these differences, and how do we interpret them? The inclusion of *ipo_year* in OLS_long exerts a significant impact on the coefficient estimates, but—perhaps more importantly—it reduces the threat of endogeneity and bias in the estimations. Both theory and the correlation matrix in Table 6.5 suggest that *ipo_year* (a time-variant variable) should be included in the regression model, but what if we cannot gather data on this variable, as in Model OLS_short? This is when panel-data estimation and *FE-models* save the day!

Step 3: Estimation of the Model, Option 2: Fixed Effects
Pooled-OLS estimation is not particularly helpful in establishing causal relationships unless stringent assumptions can be met. One of these assumptions relates to the absence of omitted correlated variables (OVCs). Unfortunately, in this

case, there are two unobservable variables because of lack of data or measurement error. A way to overcome or at least minimize these issues is to employ FE estimation. FE exploits the longitudinal nature of the data to control for unobservable factors in regression models. FE is particularly suitable when the source of heterogeneity is *time-invariant*–that is, it belongs to the same individual over time and differs only between individuals (e.g., a person's place of birth) [11]. In order to perform an FE estimation to address the original research question, the model in (Eq. 6.4: FE) is specified:

FE:

$$
\begin{aligned}
Mkt\_cap_{it} = \alpha_0 &+ \beta_1 rd\_exp\_chg_{it} + \beta_2 founder_{it} + \beta_3 bod\_size_{it} \\
&+ \beta_4 ipo\_year_i + v_{it}
\end{aligned}
\tag{6.4}
$$

The FE model differs from OLS_short and OLS_long pooled specifications in the addition of a time component (t in the subscript), which indicates that the value of observed variables changes between individuals but also within individuals over time. In essence, FE models provide estimation coefficients that are the average of the *within-individuals* effects on the outcome variable (in this case, $N = 20$, so 20 estimations are computed and averaged). Therefore, variables that do not change at an individual level are not taken into account. *ipo_year* does not vary within units but only between units, so β_4 is not estimated. Likewise, the component of the error term that is time-invariant (μ_i) has a mean that corresponds to the value of the individual observations, so the between-units error is not taken into account. These differences, although they border on abstract, are useful in assessing the differences between FE and RE models.

Table 6.7 reports results from the pooled-OLS and FE estimations. Since FE does not estimate any coefficient on the time-invariant variables, *ipo_year* is not estimated. (FE models estimate within-unit changes, so if there is no change, no estimation is returned.) The coefficients in the two models are different: The effect of *rd_exp_chg* on market capitalization becomes much smaller (3.11 vs. 5.07) when FE is employed than when OLS is used because FE estimation computes within-individual changes and returns an average of these effects. *bod_size* does not affect *mkt_cap* in the FE model, although it has a positive effect in OLS. Similarly, the positive effect of *founder* on *mkt_cap* in OLS is smaller but statistically significant in the FE model versus OLS (6.84 vs. 9.20). Therefore, we infer that estimates from the pooled-OLS model on the three predictors were misleading, the product of their correlation with unobserved firm-specific factors that also impact market capitalization.[9]

The FE model accounts for unobserved heterogeneity that relates to *time-invariant* variables, but this gain in terms of *unbiasedness* comes at a cost, as FE does not

---

[9]FE models control for all of the time-invariant factors that affect the relationship of interest, whereas OLS takes into account only the covariates that are available. In this example, there are unobservable variables that affect X and Y that FE estimation takes into account but OLS ignores. Since FE estimation is always less biased than OLS, it is preferable.

Table 6.7 Comparison of OLS and FE models

DV: *mkt_cap*	Model OLS_long		FE model	
	Coeff (se)	*t*	Coeff (se)	*T*
rd_exp_chg	5.07 (2.36)	2.15	3.11 (0.54)	5.71
bod_size	6.41 (1.93)	3.33	0.81 (0.67)	1.33
founder	9.20 (7.37)	1.25	6.84 (1.71)	4.01
ipo_year	−4.69 (0.76)	−6.16	Omitted	
intercept	9483 (1539)	6.16	148 (5.42)	27.33
Adj-R	0.83			
F-test	121 ($p < 0.001$)			
N			100	
N (groups)			20	
Overall-R^2			0.23	
within-R^2			0.53	
between-R^2			0.51	
corr (μ_i; Xb)			0.42	
F-test (μ_i $= 0$)			214.92 ($p < 0.001$)	
rho			0.99	

take into account variables that do not change at an individual level, so they systematically underestimate the model. In fact the adjusted R^2 for OLS2 is much larger than the equivalent for the FE model (e.g., the within-$R^2 = 0.53$).

FE models offer a battery of diagnostic tests that allow researchers to make an overall assessment of the estimation's suitability. These tests are displayed in Table 6.7. The conventional test-statistics reported in OLS estimation:

- The number of firm-year observations (N = 100) should be accompanied by an indication of the number of groups (N = 20).
- Instead of reporting a unique indication of model fit, as in OLS regression (Adjusted R^2), FE models partition it into three components: an overall R^2 (0.23) that rarely exceeds 0.60 unless within-variance is very high, a within-R^2 (0.53) that is usually reported in FE models, and a between-R^2 (0.51) that is of limited usefulness in FE.
- An important diagnostic is corr (μ_i; Xb), which indicates the magnitude of the correlation between omitted unobservable variables and the error term. It tests the relevance of the individually specific heterogeneity in relation to the variables in the model. In this case, the correlation is high (0.42), so individual-level differences are relevant.
- The F-test (μ_i $= 0$) diagnoses whether individual effects are present. Rejecting the null hypothesis implies that observations are nested, that firm-level characteristics matter, and that panel data should be preferred to OLS. In this case, the model returns a high value (214.92; $p < 0.001$), so the FE model should be preferred.

- The *rho* indicator is an *intra-class coefficient* that suggests whether the twenty groups (each firm) are consistent internally. In this case, homogeneity is high ($rho = 0.99$).

Step 3: Estimation of the Model, Option 3: Random Effects

We have discussed the FE model as a specific estimation for panel data. By ignoring between-individual variation, FE attenuates concerns with time-invariant individually specific heterogeneity in the estimation of the X on Y. Despite this significant advantage, FE models are limited because they ignore sources of variation and do not offer estimations of the time-invariant variables on the outcome. *Random-effects models* (RE models) are the main competitors of FE. The main difference between these models and FE models lies in RE's ability to take into account both within- and between-individual variation, so it offers coefficient estimates for the time-invariant variables (e.g., *ipo_year* in our current example).

In order to explain the logic of RE estimation and compare it with FE and OLS models, we employ the same example in which our main question of interest concerns whether R&D expenses affect market capitalization. Performing an *RE model* estimation requires specifying the model in (Eq. 6.5: RE):

RE:

$$
\begin{aligned}
Mkt\_cap_{it} = {} & \alpha_0 + \beta_1 rd\_exp\_chg_{it} + \beta_2 founder_{it} + \beta_3 bod\_size_{it} \\
& + \beta_4 ipo\_year_i + \upsilon_{it}
\end{aligned}
\tag{6.5}
$$

(Eq. 6.5: RE) is identical to (Eq. 6.4: FE), given that both FE and RE models belong to the family of panel-data estimation methods. However, there are two key differences: unlike FE estimations, the RE models provide a coefficient estimate on *ipo_year* (coefficient β_4), and RE models make assumptions about the distribution of the between-individual component of the error term (μ_i).

Table 6.8 reports results from an RE estimation of the model specified in (Eq. 6.5: RE). As this example shows:

- RE models report a test of statistical significance in the form of Z-values rather than *t*-values, but their interpretation is identical.
- RE estimates a coefficient for *ipo_year* that is missing in the FE estimation. This coefficient is negative (-6.65; $p < 0.001$), so firms that list later (2014 vs. 2005) display decreasing levels of R&D expenses.
- The overall R^2 of the model is large, indicating that the inclusion of a time-invariant covariate significantly improves the model estimation.
- The correlation between the between-individual portion of the error (μ_1) and the omitted covariates is assumed to be 0. This assumption was not considered in the FE model estimation, where we estimated a value for this coefficient.

Table 6.8 Random-
effects estimation

DV: *mkt_cap*	RE model	
	Coeff (se)	z
rd_exp_chg	3.11 (0.55)	5.69
bod_size	0.91 (0.61)	1.49
founder	6.83 (1.71)	3.98
ipo_year	−6.65 (0.79)	−8.44
intercept	13464 (1578)	8.53
N	100	
N (groups)	20	
overall-R^2	0.81	
within-R^2	0.53	
between-R^2	0.82	
corr (μ_i; X)	Assumed = 0	
Wald-χ^2	172.77 ($p < 0.001$)	
rho	0.97	

6.5   When to Use OLS, Fixed-Effects, and Random-Effects Models

Now that we have illustrated and discussed the mechanics of pooled-OLS models and both FE and RE models, the next question of interest concerns *which estimation technique should be employed in which analysis*. The chances of getting close to the right choice lies more in a researcher's knowledge of the theory and mechanisms behind the variables of interest than in the data, let alone the choice of statistical tool. The choice of the right model can be split into choosing between pooled OLS on one hand and FE and RE models on the other, and if FE and RE models are chosen, choosing between them.

Pooled OLS vs. Fixed- and Random-Effects Models

While panel-data estimations are better suited than the OLS to estimating relationships in data sets that feature *repeated observations*, under certain circumstances pooled-OLS estimations are a valid (and less costly) alternative to RE and FE models. For example, in the (unlikely) event that we can gather data such that a series of covariates are added to the model, we need not worry about the potential for omitted correlated variables; in this instance, pooled OLS works just fine. To help make this decision, we can determine whether our data allows us to add a series of covariates to the model using the *Breusch-Pagan Lagrange multiplier test* (also known as the Breusch-Pagan test). This test evaluates the following hypotheses:

H_0: *Var* $(\mu_i) = 0$
H_a: *Var* $(\mu_1) > 0$

The Breusch-Pagan test indicates whether variance in individual-level observations is similar across the sample[10]; if this is the case, one can ignore the nestedness of the data and see each observation as independent. Failing to reject the H_0 (e.g. $p > 0.05$) indicates that pooled OLS is a valid alternative to the panel-data estimation, while rejecting the null hypothesis)indicates that individual variation matters and panel-data models should be employed.

Running a Breusch-Pagan test in STATA involves two steps [12]: estimating an RE model, including all the time-invariant variables, and using the *xttest0* routine to test the H_0: Var $(\mu_i) = 0$. In the ad-hoc example we are using (e.g., *do R&D expenses enhance a company's market value?*), the results follow:

Test: Var(u) = 0

$X^2 = 164.84$ Prob $> X^2 = 0.0000$

These values prompt a rejection of the null hypotheses (i.e., pooled-OLS and panel-data are equivalent) because of the relevance of the within-unit variance. The next step involves choosing between RE and FE models.

Fixed-Effects vs. Random-Effects Models

Once we have determined that we prefer panel-data estimation to pooled-OLS estimation, the next question concerns whether we prefer *fixed-effects or random-effects estimation*. Given that both approaches have their advantages and limitations, an ex-ante suggestion should not be warranted in terms of one approach's being superior to the other. In order to be effective, both models must meet underlying assumptions that can be verified by employing estimation routines that statistical software embeds in their toolkits.[11]

One way to look at the decision is to consider that RE models are efficient in estimation, whereas FE models are less biased than RE models. While both features are desirable, it is difficult to achieve both. RE models have an advantage in their employment of a richer information set than FE via the estimation of coefficients on all variables, both time-variant and time-invariant, which improves model estimation. In the previous example (see Table 6.8), the RE model returns an estimation coefficient for *ipo_year* that is omitted in the FE model. Nevertheless, RE suffers from a severe omitted correlated variable bias if between-individual variation in the outcome variable is due to numerous unobservable factors. FE estimation eludes these factors–at least the time-invariant ones–so it provides less biased results.

How do we determine whether RE or FE is more suitable? Given the impossibility of observing the extent of the bias that is due to OCVs, we follow an empirical strategy offered by the Hausman [13]. The *Hausman test* indicates whether the coefficients of two models (RE and FE) differ. The null hypothesis)in Hausman tests is that there are no systematic differences:

Test: H_0: The difference in coefficients is not systematic.

---

[10]The key objective of the Breusch-Pagan test is understanding whether one cand discard the clustering that is due to the same individuals being included multiple times.

[11]For the sake of consistency, will refer to the STATA estimation routines.

Failing to reject the null hypothesis suggests that the coefficients are close enough not to be considered different. In this situation, the RE model is preferred because of the gain in efficiency without facing the risk of biasedness. By contrast, rejecting the null hypothesis suggests that the differences are systematic, and FE estimation should be employed.

Running a Hausman test in STATA involves four steps [12]:

1. Estimate the RE model, including all the time-invariant variables that will be dropped in the FE model. Then store the coefficients in the memory using the command *estimates store* (RE_model).
2. Estimate the FE model and store the coefficients in the memory using the command *estimates store* (FE_model).
3. Employ the estimation command *"hausman"* as *hausman FE_model RE_model*.
4. Compare the test statistics to determine whether the null-hypothesis is rejected.

Table 6.9 provides the results from the data from our running example.

Table 6.9 shows that the RE model provides a negative coefficient on the time-invariant variable *ipo_year*. Other coefficients are similar in terms of both magnitude and significance levels, a reassuring result because the estimations converge. Nevertheless, the null hypothesis)of no differences between coefficients is rejected in the Hausman test ($\chi^2 = 13.93$, $p < 0.0001$), so given the closeness between coefficients, the choice of one model over the other one would not make much difference in this example.[12]

A Toolkit for Choosing the Most Appropriate Estimation Model

Figure 6.2 offers a graphic representation of the steps in choosing whether pooled-OLS estimation or panel-data estimation is more suitable. First, the Breusch-Pagan test reveals whether the pooled-OLS estimation is a valid estimation strategy. Then, if panel-data estimation is preferable, the Hausman test indicates whether an RE model or an FE model offers the more efficient and less biased strategy.

To wrap up our example, Table 6.10 compares the estimation results from three models (OLS_long, FE, and RE). All models have a good overall fit with the data, with R^2 consistently larger than 0.50, but there are some notable differences: First, OLS overestimates the magnitude of the effect of *R&D expenses* on *market capitalization* relative to the FE and RE estimations. The Breusch-Pagan test offered a clear indication that panel-data estimation should be preferred to pooled-OLS estimation because of the within-firm variability that should be taken into account and because of the presence of unobservable factors (both time-variant and time-invariant).

---

[12]A note of caution when employing Hausman test: Results of the test are limited to the *specific models fitted with FE and RE*. They are not intended as a definitive response to whether we should employ FE or RE to answer the research question of interest. Changing the specification of FE or RE models by adding different covariates will lead to different results. It is good practice to re-estimate different models and compare them before making any statement or decisions.

Table 6.9 Comparing RE and FE models with the Hausman test

	FE model		RE model	
DV: *mkt_cap*	Coeff (se)	*t*	Coeff (se)	*z*
rd_exp_chg	3.11 (0.54)	5.7	3.11 (0.55)	5.69
bod_size	0.81 (0.67)	1.33	0.91 (0.61)	1.49
founder	6.84 (1.71)	4	6.83 (1.71)	3.98
ipo_year	Omitted		−6.65 (0.79)	−8.44
intercept	148 (5.42)	27.33	13464 (1578)	8.53
N	100		100	
N (groups)	20		20	
overall-R	0.23		0.81	
within-R	0.53		0.53	
between-R	0.51		0.82	
corr (μ; Xb)	0.42		Assumed = 0	
Wald-X	214.92 ($p < 0.001$)		172.77 ($p < 0.001$)	
rho	0.99		0.97	

Hausman test result: Differences in coefficients are not systematic.

$X^2 = 13.93$

$\text{Prob} > \chi^2 = 0.000$

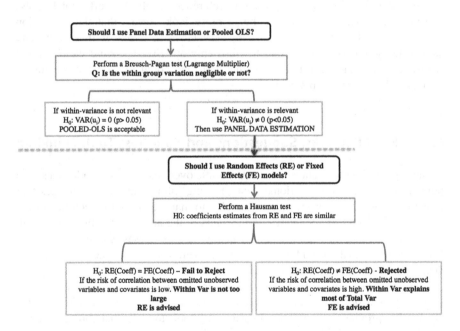

Fig. 6.2 A process for choosing the most appropriate estimation model

Table 6.10 Comparison of pooled-OLS, FE, and RE models

DV: *mkt_cap*	Model OLS_long		FE model		RE model	
	Coeff (se)	t	Coeff (se)	t	Coeff (se)	z
rd_exp_chg	5.07 (2.36)	2.15	3.11 (0.54)	5.7	3.11 (0.55)	5.69
bod_size	6.41 (1.93)	3.33	0.81 (0.67)	1.33	0.91 (0.61)	1.49
Founder	9.20 (7.37)	1.25	6.84 (1.71)	4	6.83 (1.71)	3.98
ipo_year	−4.69 (0.76)	−6.16	Omitted		−6.65 (0.79)	−8.44
Intercept	9483 (1539)	6.16	148 (5.42)	27.33	13464 (1578)	8.53
Adj-R	0.83					
F-test	121 ($p < 0.001$)					
N			100		100	
N (groups)			20		20	
overall-R			0.23		0.81	
within-R			0.53		0.53	
between-R			0.51		0.82	
corr (μ; Xb)			0.42		Assumed = 0	
Wald-X			214.92 ($p < 0.001$)		172.77 ($p < 0.001$)	
Rho			0.99		0.97	

Next, the Hausman test suggested a preference for the less efficient but less biased estimation, the FE model, but a close look reveals that the estimation coefficients in FE and RE models are very close in terms of magnitude and statistical significance. Given that RE also employs *time-invariant* variables and returns an estimation coefficient, in this case one could rely on the RE model instead of FE-model (Table 6.11).

6.6   Final Remarks, Suggestions and Your Best Tool: Thinking!

Gathering longitudinal data is always preferable over observations made at a single point in time (i.e., cross-sectional data). Having information about changes that affect units over time or even just being able to map trends and trajectories of the phenomena of interest adds value and insights to the analysis. On the other hand, collecting longitudinal data is more costly and increases the complexity in handling, manipulating, and analyzing data. Overall, however, the advantages of dealing with longitudinal data outweigh the costs.

Once the data are there, the next issue to address concerns *what estimation strategy is best suited to answering the research question of interest.* We hope this chapter has provided you with all the necessary tools to make that choice. Keep in mind, however, that there is no one superior estimation strategy a priori, as choosing the best statistical technique is a function of the characteristics of the data collected. Every choice—pooled-OLS models, FE models, or RE models—has its shortcomings and limitations: The best strategy is to evaluate all of them and make an informed decision for the specific case you are examining.

Table 6.11 Comparison of estimation models

	Pooled OLS	Fixed effects	Random effects
Within-variance	Not taken into account	Estimates the effect of X on Y considering the individually specific time-invariant factors	When the Hausman test is favorable or the impact of time constant X on Y is worth being taken into consideration
Between-variance	Not taken into account	Unobserved time-invariant OVCs are a concern.	Effect of the time constant X on Y
Time-invariant unobserved effects	Not controlled for	Controlled for	Partially controlled for
Main limitations	1. Does not recognize that observations come from the same units 2. Does not account for OVC	Does not estimate time-invariant covariates (inefficient use of data)	Does not explicitly remove endogeneity that occurs because of time-invariant variables (biasedness of estimation)
When should be used	Only if one can retrieve all covariates to minimize endogeneity concerns	1. Groups are homogeneous and variation comes from within groups. 2. Between-variance is not relevant.	The amount of unobservable time-invariant heterogeneity is not relevant.
Advantages	Easy to implement and interpret	Removes unobserved sources of heterogeneity if omitted variables are time-invariant	Makes the best use of data, though should not be used when within-variance is relevant

When you are reporting the results, disclosing the chosen strategy and the detailed decisions at length, together with the potential limitations of the choice, will reassure the reader. Finally, it is a good idea to share results–or at least discuss them–from all angles (i.e., model specifications). If there is convergence, the reader's concerns will be reduced, and if there is divergence (as in most of our examples), a detailed discussion will strengthen the validity of your results.

References

1. Wooldridge JM (2002) Econometric analysis of cross section and panel data. MIT Press, Cambridge, MA
2. Gow ID, Ormazabal G, Taylor DJ (2010) Correcting for cross-sectional and time-series dependence in accounting research. Account Rev 85(2):483–512
3. Cameron A, Trivedi P (2009) Microeconometrics: methods and applications. Cambridge University Press, New York, NY
4. Petersen MA (2009) Estimating standard errors in finance panel data sets: comparing approaches. Rev of Financ Stud 22:435–480

5. Enders W (2008) Applied econometric times series. Wiley, New York
6. Baltagi B (2014) Panel data econometrics. Routledge, London
7. White H (1980) A heteroscedasticity-consistent covariance matrix estimator and a direct test for heteroscedasticity. Econometrica 48:817–838
8. Fama EF, MacBeth JD (1973) Risk, return, and equilibrium: empirical tests. J Polit Econ 81:607–636
9. Newey WK, West KD (1987) A simple, positive semi-definite, heteroscedasticity and auto-correlation consistent covariance matrix. Econometrica 55:703–708
10. Peel M (2014) Addressing unobserved endogeneity bias in accounting studies: control and sensitivity methods by variable type. Account Bus Res 44:545–571
11. Cameron CA, Gelbach JB, Miller DJ (2009) Robust inference with multiway clustering. J Bus Econ Stat 29:238–249
12. Thompson S (2011) Simple formulas for standard errors that cluster by both firm and time. J Fin Econ 99:1–10
13. Hausman JA (1978) Specification tests in econometrics. Econometrica 46:1251–1271

Causality: Endogeneity Biases and Possible Remedies

7

Many, if not all, studies in accounting and information systems address causal research questions. A key feature of such questions is that they seek to establish whether a variation in X (the treatment) leads to a state change in Y (the effect). These studies go beyond an association between two phenomena (i.e., a correlation between variables in the empirical model) to find a true cause-effect relationship. Moving from a simple association to a causal claims requires meeting a number of conditions.

Consider the relationship between board independence and firm performance. A recurrent question concerns whether increasing board independence (cause) improves decision-making or firm performance (effect). Addressing this question involves several methodological issues that, if ignored, hamper the ability to make conclusive claims about the cause-effect relationship. In order to address this question, the research design should take into account two issues: Firm performance or expected performance may affect a board's choice in appointing more or less independent directors (an example of reverse causality), and the number of independent directors varies with a number of other variables that jointly affect the main predictor and the effect of interest (an example of omitted correlated variables).

So far, we have introduced several statistical methods with which to investigate relationships between variables. This chapter examines the conditions an empirical study has to meet in order to support causal claims. In so doing, the chapter compares an ideal state (e.g., a randomized experiment) with non-experimental data and discusses the issues researchers encounter in dealing with observational data. Then it offers a hands-on approach to a series of remedies to overcome the potential shortcomings in designing or executing research that seeks to make causal claims.

© Springer International Publishing Switzerland 2017
W. Mertens et al., *Quantitative Data Analysis*, DOI 10.1007/978-3-319-42700-3_7

7.1   Your Research Question Is Causal: What Does that Mean?

Imagine you have collected data that shows an increase in a technology's perceived usefulness and intent to use the technology. It would be tempting to state that perceived usefulness *caused* that increase in intent to use (and that is often how scholars report such results). However, there are at least three reasons that such a conclusion is probably premature: First, that two things occur together or behave similarly (i.e., co-vary) is not sufficient reason to conclude that one variable causes another. They may have co-varied by chance or because of a third variable that influenced both. Second, a causal conclusion like this is allowed only when cases (people) are randomly assigned to different levels of the independent variable (perceived usefulness), when that independent variable is manipulated in a controlled environment (e.g., by assigning them to technologies that are, in fact, more or less useful), and when the manipulation precedes the effect in time (i.e., when we measure the intent to use *after* they developed their perceptions of usefulness). This point is critical because most of our studies rely at least in part on self-selection or are plagued by other selection biases; rarely include an opportunity to manipulate the levels of an independent variable, let alone in controlled environments; and often collect measures at one point in time rather than at multiple points in time (most evident in cross-sectional surveys). Third, simultaneous measurements, selection bias, and lack of controlled manipulation also mean that many other variables vary between cases and co-vary with relevant variables, and some of these influence the results.

For these three reasons, we must design studies so they avoid these problems, understand the cause and size of these problems if they do emerge despite our efforts, and deal with them accordingly while analyzing the data and reporting results. This is what this chapter is about.

This chapter is especially relevant to you if you answer "yes" to two questions:

(1) Is your research question causal (i.e., you are investigating whether, by changing the quantity or state in X, a change in state or quantity in Y is expected)?
(2) Is your data non-experimental and non-randomly assigned to the conditions (e.g., observational data from secondary sources, archival sources, or a survey instrument)?

If you answered yes to both questions, you cannot simply compare the outcomes (Y) across dimensions of X to establish a causal relationship (X affects Y). To put it bluntly, you should not use data collected at one point in time to make statements like "increases in perceived usefulness increases intentions to use." If your research question is causal but your units are not randomly assigned to the control and treatment conditions or to different levels of treatment, then you need to *think before you act*!

Most empirical issues that hamper researchers' ability to make *causal claims* stem from the fact that individuals/groups/firms can *choose* to adopt or follow certain behaviors–our treatment of interest. In addition, their choice is driven by factors that affect the outcome variable as well [1]. For example, firms *choose* the level of board independence , so a host of factors that affected the choice contemporaneously impact the outcomes [2]. Therefore, observed units that choose their (level of) "treatment" are systematically different from those that do not, and if such **self-selection** is based on attributes that affect the outcome variable (Y), then our analyses will be biased. Furthermore, researchers often observe only the outcome of the choice made but not the outcome that would have occur had an alternative choice *been made* [3].

For example, imagine you wish to test whether board independence (X, the treatment) affects the quality of financial information (Y, the effect). The choice of having zero, a few, or many independent directors on the board is voluntary and not randomly assigned. Firms choose to set up their own boards within the boundaries of regulatory requirements according to a series of internal features and needs. In empirical terms, firms across different levels of X (i.e., board independence) are not *equal* in terms of the expected outcome (i.e., quality of financial information) prior to their choice of the level of board independence. Large and highly profitable firms tend to appoint more independent directors and deliver high-quality financial information. Therefore, failing to take into account firm size in our empirical design results in overestimating the effect of board independence on the quality of financial information. (For example, larger boards tend to be more independent, so the two factors should be disentangled.)

The board example illustrates a causal question that many researchers have tried to address with non-experimental data, as it is difficult to find a sufficient number of boards that will allow their level of board independence to be manipulated for the sake of research. While non-random data allows an association between board independence and financial reporting quality to be claimed, the researcher is not in a position to substantiate causality.

After identifying a relevant research question, we should identify the most appropriate method or technique with which to address it. The nature of the claims we seek to substantiate significantly affect our choices [4]. Seeking to establish an *effect* or the *impact* of a treatment on an observable outcome entails a series of choices in terms of data collection and analysis that minimizes the risk of alternative explanations (i.e., counterfactuals) and endogeneity issues [5]. Endogeneity means that the values of the main predictor across units come from within the model, so the estimated coefficients are biased because of a correlation of the error term with the predictors. Planning is important to ensuring that the empirical strategy allows the causal claims one seeks to substantiate to be supported or not.

A first step in such planning entails having a thorough look at the theoretical predictions [6]. No empirical methods or techniques will (ex-post) suffice to overcome methodological concerns without a sound (ex-ante) understanding of the mechanisms that affect the relationships of interest. Theory dictates model specification and, in turn, analysis: no statistics expert will find something meaningful in the data without solid theoretical guidance.

The reminder of the chapter addresses these issues, with the intent of increasing researchers' awareness of the problems at stake identifying the right tools.

Conditions for Drawing Causal Conclusions: The Ideal State(s)

When researchers seek to establish whether one variable (X) exerts an effect on another variable (Y), they seek to make a causal claim. The challenge lies in assessing whether, at different levels of X and with *everything else held constant* the outcome variable (Y) changes and by how much. One of the most significant hurdles in accounting and information systems is drawing valid conclusions based on the observed phenomena [7]. Two issues are particularly important: internal validity and external validity. Internal Validity refers to the unambiguity with which we draw conclusions about the relationships and mechanisms identified in our study by ruling out alternative explanations. Internal validity points to the certainty with which we can claim that the changes in Y are due to the variation of X. External Validity relates to the generalizability of the results beyond our setting. Once we make sure that results are internally valid, we must determine whether the conditions are specific and local to the setting or are applicable to other contexts.

A rich literature offers detailed guidance in terms of making causal inferences in the field of social science [8, 9]. Mills established three conditions for causal inference: The cause (X) should precede the effect (Y) temporally; the change in the treatment (X) should produce a change in the effect (Y); and the observed change in the effect should be *unequivocally* attributed to the treatment (i.e., no other potentially confounding causes).

The first condition—that the cause (X) should precede the effect (Y) temporally—highlights the need for clear temporal sequencing: the treatment must precede the effect such that the manifestation and measurement of X occurs before Y. This requirement has consequences on studies that rely on survey instruments, interviews, or questionnaires, where information about the main predictor and information the outcome are often (but not always) acquired at the same time. One of the shortcomings of such data relate to the researcher's limited ability to discern the temporal logic through which the observed phenomena occurred.

The second condition—that a change in X produces a change in Y—means only that individuals/groups/firms that are subject to a treatment should differ significantly from otherwise similar units that are not subject to the treatment.

The third condition—that the observed change in Y should be *unequivocally attributed* to the change in X—is the most difficult to ensure, as it requires that no other concurrent factors exert an influence on the variation in Y, so the change can be *attributed* to the hypothesized cause. In experimental research, this principle rules out alternative hypotheses, but outside of experiments, the nature of the phenomenon and the means of observation and measurement can make it difficult to ensure that no other *causes* affect the outcome variable. For example, changes in regulation at a macro level (e.g., the adoption of new accounting standards) or at a micro level (e.g., a change in organizational structure) hardly come on their own but are themselves influenced by many factors. Therefore, it is difficult to ensure that no concurrent forces affect the variation in Y.

Bearing these three conditions in mind prior to the design of the study ensures the data can support making causal claims. A good practice entails understanding the ideal state or conditions required to claim *causality* and benchmarking the ideal state with the realistic conditions and data availability. An example is offered by studies on the impact on firm value of granting stock options (SO) to the CEO [10]. Finance theory suggests that alignment of interests between stockholders and managers in publicly listed companies reduces agency costs by directing CEOs' efforts toward maximizing shareholder value [11]. Whether and to what extent this approach translates into positive gains for shareholders are empirical questions. In an *ideal state* one would measure the effects of giving SO to CEOs as the difference between the market value of company Alpha (MV_A) under the two conditions: (1) the CEO of Alpha is given a SO plan (SO_1), or (2) the CEO of Alpha is not given a SO plan (SO_0). Hence:

$$EFFECT = (MV_A | SO_1) - (MV_A | SO_0) \tag{7.1}$$

In this case, we compare two hypothetical states: the market value (MV) of Alpha at $T = 1$ (MV_A) once the SO plan has been granted at $T = 0$, and a *counterfactual*–the market value of Alpha at time $T = 1$ if the SO plan had not been granted at $T = 0$. In reality, Alpha either grants a SO plan or not, so we cannot observe both states. In both conditions, we would miss a counterfactual so no causal claim is possible in theory unless we have a *time machine* that enables us to observe one state (e.g., SO is given to the CEO), measure market value, and then go back in time, modify the treatment condition (e.g., the CEO is *not* given a SO), and measure market value. We have to resort other solutions. The issue then becomes how to identify a valid counterfactual.

Econometrics textbooks offer plenty of solutions [4, 12]. One involves identifying a (group of) firms that resemble Alpha as much as possible (e.g., in terms of size, industry, profitability, governance) **and** that differ uniquely in terms of their choice of giving (or not) a SO plan to the CEO. The best route involves employing randomized experiments that assign a group of companies to the *treatment* condition (SO_1) and another group of companies to the *control* condition (SO_0). A significant advantage of randomized experiments is that they minimize self-selection bias; in other words, we would not let firms *choose whether to give a SO plan to their* CEOs; instead, firms are assigned to either condition. If we were able to do so, we would be able to assess the effects of granting stock option as:

$$EFFECT = (MV | SO_1) - (MV | SO_0) \tag{7.2}$$

In this case, we observe both states and compare groups of similar firms randomly assigned to the SO condition (treatment group) or not (control group). Thus we can see the effect of the treatment by comparing the average MV of the treatment and control groups. Since firms are randomly assigned to either of the two conditions, there is no reason to suspect that the two groups are significantly different (between-groups variation) along any dimension. Differences within the two groups (within-group variation) do not affect or bias our conclusions.

The gold standard for causal studies is an experimental condition in which all factors are held constant [3]. Unfortunately, such a condition is difficult, if not impossible, to achieve with observational data alone, so the strength and quality of the claims we make are affected. Failing to isolate the effects of the main predictor on the outcome of interest increases the risk of mis-attributing the effect to other concurrent factors.

A Reality Check: Dealing with Observational, Non-Randomized Data
Understanding the conditions required to support causal claims and why *randomized experiments* get us close to these conditions being realistic about the nature of the data we deal with in a researcher's domain and why they are problematic. Unfortunately, manipulating the observed phenomena and the confounds that *cause* the changes we see is difficult, and the time machines we need remain remote. In general, accessing a limited set of the data while neglecting other and perhaps more promising sources of information makes research bounded. In these situations, one solution is to develop a study design that puts us in a condition *as if we were* in a randomized experiment.

Going back to the previous question concerning whether granting SO to CEOs affects a firm value, if you were to ask a large number of firms to grant their CEOs SO plans (the treatment group) and a comparable group of firms to refrain from giving their CEOs SO plans (the control group), you would be unlikely to gain consent. Even if you did, you would have reason to doubt the quality of firms that are willing to make such an important choice in support of research.

Some firms choose to grant SO plans to their CEO, while others do not. Since this choice is voluntary, it depends on a number of factors, and it is these other factors that constrain our ability to assign firms to the treatment or control conditions. Two groups of firms that choose to grant or not grant SO to their CEOs does not meet the *equality in expectations* condition that must be met to allow causal claims.

For example, firms that grant SO plans to their CEOs are often wealthier and more profitable than those who do not, so companies that offer SO plans tend to have higher MV. Hence, analyses will be biased, resulting in *overestimating* the effects of SO plans on MV, inflated by ex-ante differences in profitability. In addition, some firms that are having difficulty may try to attract CEOs by ensuring them more-than-proportional remuneration if they manage a turnaround. CEOs may be willing to accept a SO plan if they foresee the opportunity to gain significant remuneration. In such scenarios, analyses will be biased because of *under-estimating* the effects SO plans exert on market valuation. Therefore, when comparing firms across levels of MV and without the possibility of random assignment to the SO-plan or no-SO-plan conditions, estimation coefficients will either over- or under-estimate the sign and magnitude of the relationships.

In order to clarify the types and sources of empirical issues in dealing with non-randomized data, the next section provides an overview of the sources of problems that relate to *self-selection issues*.

7.2   Self-Selection and Endogeneity

"Selection occurs when observations are non-randomly sorted into discrete groups, resulting in the potential coefficient bias in estimation procedures such as OLS" [13].

The difficulty in getting close to the ideal state requires taking into account a number of issues when dealing with observational data and the treatment is non-randomly assigned to units. Two expressions are particularly important: *self-selection* and *endogeneity bias*. The self-selection problem relates to the (violation of) independence of observations. A condition of causal interpretation is that observations are similar along a number of dimensions except on the treatment or main predictor (X). Self-selection problems occur when observed units choose to follow (adopt) certain rules (behaviors), and the self-selection is based on attributes that affect the outcome variable. Thus, units that choose a certain behavior (the treatment group) are systematically different from those that don't (the control group). If the selection is based on attributes that affect the outcome variable, then analyses will be biased.

Self-selection leads to a series of *endogeneity concerns* that affect many of our studies.[1] We discuss four of these concerns: omitted correlated variables (observable and unobservable), reverse causality, and simultaneity.

Omitted Correlated Variables

Omitted correlated variables (OCVs) describe situations in which a variable that exerts an effect on both X and Y is *omitted* from the empirical model. A classic example in economics is the relationship between levels of education and future earnings, where parents' wealth affects **both** the likelihood of getting additional education and future earnings. OCVs arise in contexts wherein the treatment (X) is non-randomly distributed across the units, as each unit chooses whether to be treated (e.g., to hire a Big-4 auditing firm or not) and/or the level of the treatment (e.g., the amount paid to the external auditor). Firms choose whether to hire a Big-4 auditor and negotiate their audit fees because of own features and needs (e.g., size, as larger companies tend to buy more assurance from auditors, and level of financial risk). If firms that choose to hire a Big-4 auditor differ in significant ways from those that do not, there is a risk of attributing the differences in the dependent variables to a confounding factor. The extent of the bias is a function of the magnitude of the correlation between the main predictor (X) and the OCV, and the size of the relationship between the OCV and the outcome variable (Y).

---

[1]Editors and reviewers are increasingly aware of the issues with observational data and causal claims. Some of the leading journals in business and management fields suggest that authors deal with endogeneity issues in the manuscript prior to the first submission of the study for consideration: http://strategicmanagement.net/pdfs/smj-guidelines-regarding-empirical-research.pdf

Fig. 7.1 Omitted correlated
variables

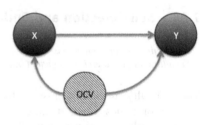

A key characteristic of potential OCVs is that the variable must *jointly* affect the choice of X (and/or its level of) *and* the dependent variable (Y). OVCs can be of two types: **observable** OVCs if the variable is available and data collection is feasible and **unobservable** OVCs if the data for this variable are not accessible or are subject to measurement flaws.

The two types of OCVs have differing statistical and econometric remedies. Figure 7.1 provides an illustration of an OCV.

Consider this example of OCVs in accounting: Several studies in accounting have sought to test whether hiring a Big-4 auditor affects the quality of accounting information, measured as the probability of receiving a going-concern opinion (*GCO*) or an internal control weakness (*ICW*) warning. Theory would predict that a Big-4 auditor enhances accounting quality because Big-4 firms are well-equipped to provide auditing assistance, and they face reputation costs in the case of audit failure. In those accounting studies, an OCV is firm size (*size*), which affects both the probability that a firm will hire a Big-4 auditing firm (e.g., large firms can afford a more expensive service) while also reducing the probability that the firm will receive a GCO, as larger firms tend to have more assets and be more established than smaller firms. Thus, failing to account for ex-ante *firm size* will result in over-estimating the effects of a Big-4 auditor on accounting quality [14]. In this instance, data on firm size is relatively easy to collect. (Total assets, market capitalization, number of employees, and turnover are all acceptable proxies for firm size.)

Unobservable OCVs could be any of many factors, including the personal attitudes or characteristics of CEOs, top management team members, or auditors. A classic example can be found in studies about the relationships between board quality (gathered through attributes like competence, size, and background) and firm performance [15]. One unobservable OCV is managerial talent, which affects both the choice of board members *and* firm performance, as skilled managers hire high-quality directors, thus leading to over-estimating the effect of boards on firm performance, or (conversely) may opt for low-quality directors, as they do not feel the urge for appointing others who may want to have a say in how the corporation is run, thus leading to under-estimating the effect of boards on firm performance. In both cases, OCVs affects the interpretation of coefficient estimates in the regression.[2]

---

[2]If a researcher could measure managerial skill with any confidence, the OCV would become observable. By adding it as a covariate to the OLS model specification, the estimation would be *freed* from the biasing effect of managerial skill.

Fig. 7.2 Reverse causality

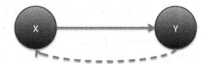

Whether there are observable or unobservable OCVs depends on the information set to which a researcher has access. Researchers focus only on observable OCVs that can be included in the model, whereas extant theory dictates which variables should be taken into account, whether they are available or not. If sources of selection come from observable attributes, then the problems are limited, but issues arise when sources of selection are unobservable [16].

Reverse Causality and Simultaneity
Another source of endogeneity in estimating coefficients is the *reverse causality* or *selection on outcome* problem [17]. Reverse causality casts doubts on the direction of the relationship: whether X affects Y or Y affects X (Fig. 7.2). An example is whether corporate transparency affects firm performance or the other way around. In accounting and information systems, managerial and firm decisions are voluntary (X, the treatment) and might be affected by concurrent or expected levels of the outcome (Y). *Simultaneity* occurs when both factors affect the other, hampering the ability to draw causal claims about the relationships of interest.

Studies in auditing commonly face reverse-causality or simultaneity issues. For example, the issue around the long-standing quest for mandatory auditor rotation concerns whether rotating external auditors improves the quality of financial reporting (e.g., by increasing auditor independence) or reduces it (e.g., by limiting the auditor's client-specific knowledge). Since auditor rotation is *voluntary*, as firms choose to renew or replace the current auditor, the issue becomes how we should interpret findings that financial-reporting quality declines with a change in auditor. A plausible interpretation is that auditor rotation reduces reporting quality because the incumbent auditor does not have the same client-specific knowledge as the outgoing auditor, but an equally plausible interpretation is that the auditor is more likely to be replaced when the financial reporting quality is low. In short, it is difficult to make clear predictions because the causality between audit rotation and the quality of financial reporting could run in either (reverse causality) or both directions (simultaneity).

7.3   Specifying OLS Models to Minimize Endogeneity Concerns

As we learned in Chap. 3, regression models are used to estimate a relationship between two or more variables. Building on the types and procedures of regression models discussed earlier, we now explain how we can specify an Ordinary Least Squares (OLS) model to minimize endogeneity concerns and get close to causal interpretation.

OLS models allow an unbiased and correct interpretation of the regression coefficients if the source of endogeneity is attributable to observable variables.[3] Understanding whether the model includes all observable variables or raises endogeneity concerns derives from a thorough knowledge of the underlying theory about what affects the main predictor and the dependent variables [18].

In regression analysis, we would normally interpret coefficient estimates on X that are significantly associated with Y as a sign of a causal relationship. However, if endogeneity exists, we cannot make such claim. This assessment does not depend on the statistical tool employed but derives from our understanding of theory. By construction, OLS estimation assumes that the error term and the predictors are not correlated, but if an omitted-variable problem or reverse-causality issue is in place, the coefficients will be biased.[4]

Take as an example a study that seeks to establish whether the ratio of outside directors on the board affects company value. The level of outside directors on the board is endogenous (i.e., a firm-level choice), which requires careful attention to the specification of OLS regression. Without careful analysis, he model specified in Eq. (7.3) is likely to return biased estimation coefficients.

$$\text{Market\_Value}_i = \alpha_0 + \alpha_1 \text{Ind\_board}_i + \varepsilon_i \qquad (7.3)$$

Two steps must be undertaken to assess the extent of the bias in Eq. (7.3): the main predictor (*ind_board*) and the outcome variable (*market_value*) should be added to augment the regression model, and we should look carefully at the correlation matrix and the correlation coefficients.

The following example mimics the available literature on board composition and market valuation to answer our research question concerning whether board independence affects firm value).[5] The structure of the data is shown in Table 7.1.

In addition to the outcome and predictor variables, a number of covariates represent potential confounding factors on the relationship of interest. Getting data on the three confounds allows us to minimize endogeneity concerns that arise from the observable factors, but we cannot control for unobservable OCVs. Given that the OLS model (Eq. 7.3) is inappropriate in light of theory, we can refine the regression model to come up with a more meaningful specification. The question is: which variables should be included and which ones can be left out

---

[3]Chapter 6 on approaches to longitudinal and panel data illustrates some additional remedies.

[4]A note of caution is warranted here. Even though OLS regression using cross-sectional data is not the best tool and setting in which to rule out endogeneity concerns, in certain circumstances researchers can still minimize endogeneity issues and rule out sources of concerns [19]. A note of thanks goes to Stefano Cascino for highlighting this sometimes hidden truth.

[5]Data and codes are available upon request from authors and will be available on the book's companion website.

Table 7.1 Descriptive statistics (board independence and firm value)

Variable	Mean	Std. dev.	Min	Max
mkt_value	267.25	134.12	40	500
ind_board	0.52	0.29	0.03	1.00
female	0.48	0.50	0	1
board_size	12.20	4.41	5	23
expert	3.03	1.40	1	5

Mkt_Value_i is the outcome variable, measured as the market capitalization at the end of the year; ind_board_i is the main predictor, which reveals the ratio of independent directors on the board; $female_i$ is a dummy variable that indicates whether at least one female director is on the board; $board\_size_i$ is the number of directors on the board; and $expert_i$ is the average level of directors' expertise in the fields of accounting or finance

without doing harm to the model? A correlation matrix is useful in answering this question. Table 7.2 shows the correlation between the variables in Table 7.1.

The correlation matrix reveals patterns in the data: First, a strong positive relationship between *ind_board* and *market value* (0.468; $p < 0.001$) lends initial support to the hypothesis that the ratio of independent board members affects the firm's market value. Next, *female* positively correlates with *market_value* (0.337; $p < 0.01$) but not with *ind_board*, while *board_size* does have a strong relationship with *ind_board* (0.406; $p < 0.001$) but not with *market_value*. Last, *acc_expert* positively correlates with both *market_value* and *ind_board*. We can draw three primary conclusions regarding how to specify the OLS model from these patterns.

1. *Accounting expertise* must be included in the OLS model because it jointly affects X (*ind_board*) and Y (*market_value*). Failing to include it will result in overestimating coefficients and misattributing a positive effect of board independence on market value, driven by accounting expertise.
2. *Female* should be included in the model. It improves the model's estimation and accuracy, as the R^2 goes up and the errors become smaller. While excluding *female* from the model does not trigger endogeneity issues, there are important gains when it is taken into account;
3. *Board size* should not be included in the model. *Board size* positively correlates with X, thus reducing the variation of the main predictor without adding much in terms of the model's explanatory power. Including it increases multicollinearity because two highly correlated variables appear to be predictors of market value (Y).

Figure 7.3 graphically depicts the variables that should be included (and not included) in a regression model based on the estimation coefficients from the correlation matrix. Equation (7.4) shows a correct OLS model for this example.

Table 7.2 Correlation matrix

	Mkt_Value	ind_board	female	board_size
ind_board	0.468	1.000		
	0.000			
female	0.337	0.041	1.000	
	0.008	0.754		
board_size	0.132	0.406	0.139	1.000
	0.316	0.001	0.290	
expert	0.480	0.692	0.001	0.164
	0.000	0.000	0.995	0.212

Mkt_Value$_i$ is the outcome variable, measured as the market capitalization at the end of the year; *ind_board$_i$* is the main predictor, which reveals the ratio of independent directors on the board; *female$_i$* is a dummy variable that indicates whether at least one female director is on the board; *board_size$_i$* is the number of directors on the board; and *expert$_i$* is the average level of directors' expertise in the fields of accounting or finance

Fig. 7.3 Selection of variables to be included in the model

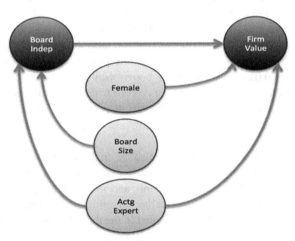

Female correlates with the DV
Board Size correlates with the IV but not with the DV
Accounting Expertise correlates with both the IV and the DV

$$\text{Market\_Value}_i = \alpha_0 + \alpha_1 \text{Ind\_board}_i + \alpha_2 \text{Expert}_i + \alpha_3 \text{Female}_i + \varepsilon_i \quad (7.4)$$

Table 7.3 compares five model specifications based on the variables included. Model 1 includes only *brd_indep* as the main predictor, and the coefficient estimate is positive and statistically significant. However, Model 1 is subject to severe endogeneity issues because of the omission of OCVs.

Model 2 adds *female* as a covariate. The estimation improves the overall fit of the model significantly (Adj-$R^2 = 30\%$), and the standard errors shrink. Notwithstanding the estimation improvement, Model 2 still suffers from potential endogeneity issues because of the omission of OCVs.

Table 7.3 Selecting covariates in OLS regression

Model	Main predictor	IV-Coeff (se)	t-stat	Covariates	Adj-R^2
1	Ind_board	216.47 (53.63)	4.04	–	0.21
2	Ind_board	210.38 (50.51)	4.16	Female	0.3
3	Ind_board	232.47 (55.25)	4.12	Female	0.29
				Board size	
4	Ind_board	109.11 (67.89)	1.61	Female	0.34
				Expert	
5	Ind_board	128.91 (74.77)	1.72	Female	0.33
				Expert	
				Board size	

Table 7.4 Selecting variables to be included in OLS model

Covariate	Main predictor	Dependent variable	Include?
Expert	Correlated	Correlated	Must be included
Brd_size	Correlated	Not correlated	Should not be included
Female	Not correlated	Correlated	Should be included

Model 3 includes both *female* and *board size*. Model 3 shows a slightly worse overall fit (Adj-$R^2 = 29\%$). Adding *board size* to the model does not harm our analysis, but multicollinearity concerns may arise. Adding covariates that do not correlate with Y but do correlate with X reduces model parsimony and magnifies standard errors.

Model 4 includes *acc_exp* because of its joint correlation with X and Y. Adding *acc_exp* to the model changes the results in reducing the size of the previously positive and significant coefficient on *brd_indep* to 109.11 and rendering it not statistically significant. On the other hand the adjusted R^2 improves to 34%.

Finally, Model 5 includes all three covariates. The results do not differ from those of Model 4, with the exception of a reduction in the adjusted R^2.

OLS allows the researcher to establish causal relationships under when the source of endogeneity is due to observable factors that can be included in the model, and there are no reverse-causality issues. Table 7.4 summarizes the decisions we can make about OLS models.

7.4 More Complex Designs to Support Causal Claims

OLS regression with covariates offers limited support for researchers' efforts to address endogeneity concerns. OLS returns coefficients based on the lack of correlation between the error term and the covariates, so it should be used only if we are sure *ex-ante* to meet this condition. In order to overcome endogeneity issues, researchers must use one of several ways to *make the main predictor exogenous*.

The first technique requires employing instrumental variable estimation [20], that is, using a set of variables (not correlated with Y) to predict X. This technique is called *first-stage regression*. A first-stage regression is employed to parcel out the exogenous portion of the main predictor prior to using it to predict the outcome of interest. A convincing implementation requires the researcher to identify exogenous predictors of X that can be excluded from the set of independent variables in the second-stage regression without raising additional endogeneity concerns [21]. This approach is employed in the *Heckman two stage procedure* and in instrumental variable estimation [22, 23].

Another common way to address endogeneity concerns is through a *matching procedure* called propensity score matching that identifies control firms that are as similar as possible to the treated ones along a number of dimensions, excluding the treatment [24].

These three approaches are explained in detail.

Instrumental Variable Estimation (IVE) and Two-Stage Least Square (2SLS)
We have shown that patterns that are evident in observational data are not definitive evidence of causal relationships; they allow one to claim association but not the direction of the association because units choose to be treated or not. As a result, X (the main predictor) is affected by other factors (OCVs) or may simultaneously change together with the outcome (Y). In both cases, endogeneity becomes a concern.

To overcome endogeneity problems, we can use *instrumental variable estimation (IVE)*. When X is endogenous, IVE employs another variable (instrument) that correlates with X but does not with the error term in the outcome model. In other words, it carves out the exogenous part from the main predictor (X) to employ it in the estimation model (*second-stage regression*). Employing the exogenous portion of X estimated by the *IV* attenuates risks of endogeneity.[6]

Inst is the instrumental variable, which shares a common area with the endogenous predictor (X) that is the portion of the predictor that is predicted by the instrument. This area can be employed in modeling the outcome variable (Y).

Figure 7.4 offers a graphic representation of what an IVE approach does: The instrumental variable and the endogenous predictor share a common area that is the portion of the predictor that is predicted by the *instrument*. This area is exogenous by definition—the instrument must not be endogenous—and can be employed in modeling the outcome variable.[7]

An IVE approach can be used if two conditions are met:

1. *Instrument* must correlate with the main predictor (X) so the *instrument* can carve out a part of the variation in X to be used as *exogenous* in predicting the

---

[6]IVE also helps in solving measurement error problems that are due to the inability to observing and measure the best proxy for the underlying concept.

[7]The portion of X (*Inst*) that is non-overlapping with *Inst* (X) is likely to be endogenous (uncorrelated with Y), so both must not be employed in estimating the outcome model.

Fig. 7.4 Endogenous regressor, instrumental variable, and outcome

outcome (Y). If the instrument and X are unrelated, there will be no overlap between the two variables that can be exploited.

2. *Instrument* must be uncorrelated with any other determinants of the dependent variable (Y) and with the error term. This necessary condition is difficult to maintain and justify: If theory suggests the *instrument* could be related to the error term in the outcome model, then the IVE approach would be simply to shift the endogeneity problem from the main predictor X to the instrument, thereby failing to deal meaningfully with it.

Meeting these conditions allows one to carve out the *exogenous* portion of X to approach a *causal* explanation of the effect of X on Y. Prior to selecting and employing an *instrument*, the researcher must justify its choice, which requires clarity and deep economic thinking. Ideally, the *instrument* should go beyond the unit's control so it can be used as a proxy for the main predictor. As a first step, *instrument* allows the main predictor, X, to be estimated as shown in (Eq. 7.5: first-stage regression).

First-stage regression:

$$X_i = \alpha_0 + \alpha_1 Instrument_i + \Sigma COV + \delta_i \tag{7.5}$$

IVE is often used in the context of a two-stage least square(2SLS) estimation, in which the endogenous regressor is "freed" from endogeneity so we can proceed with an unbiased estimation. If the *instrument* is valid and it has predictive ability, the fitted values of the main predictors $(\widehat{X})$ will be employed in the second-stage regression to estimate the outcome model, as shown in (Eq. 7.6: second-stage regression).

Second-stage regression:

$$Y_i = \beta_0 + \beta_1 \hat{X}_t + \Sigma COV + \varepsilon_i \tag{7.6}$$

In the second-stage regression, employing fitted values of the main predictor $(\widehat{X})$ attenuates endogeneity concerns in the estimation of Y.

While appealing and intuitive, it is difficult to find truly exogenous instruments. However, failing to identify and justify the choice of an instrument will result in the endogeneity problems faced with X. In this respect, the *first-stage regression* is important in assessing the validity of the IVE approach.

Researchers are confronted with a series of issues related to justifying the empirical model: First, the *validity* of the *instrument* must be assessed using any of a number of tests to ascertain whether an IVE approach is needed and the suitability of the *instrument*. For example, the *Wu-Hausman test* assesses the extent of endogeneity threat and tests whether IVE is superior to OLS in returning unbiased coefficients by comparing coefficient estimates in OLS and IVE models.[8]

A recurrent problem with IVE is the use of *weak instruments* (i.e., variables that weakly correlate to the X), reducing the variability of the fitted values in the second-stage model and challenging the suitability of the instrument as a substitute for the predictor (X). One way to detect a weak instrument is if the F-test in the first-stage regression is low.[9] A weak instrument is not a valid substitute for the endogenous regressor (X), so it should not be used.

Another issue with IVE relates to the instruments in the first stage that are excluded from the second stage (i.e., *exclusion restrictions*). Identification tests can determine whether the first-stage model is under- or over-identified and reveal whether the first stage includes (or omits) variables that should be taken out of (or included in) the estimation. Identification tests (e.g., Anderson's LM or Sargan's test) should be conducted prior to the *Wu-Hausman test*, as if the instruments are not appropriate, there is no reason to proceed with an IVE approach and no need to assess whether IVE is preferred over OLS.

Good instruments are offered by "natural experiments" [25], that is, events that affect the treatment while leaving all other variables unaltered. Studies in the governance field of sudden deaths of CEOs or unforeseen changes to regulations are examples. For instance, Armstrong, Core, and Guay employ regulatory changes that affect board composition–therefore, they are not firm-level decisions–to answer the question concerning whether *board independence improves firm transparency* [26]. Armstrong, Core, and Guay used the passing of the Sarbanes and Oxley Act in the US in 2002 to carve out the exogenous portion of changes in board independence and then used that portion to predict the effects in terms of firm transparency.

Applying IVE Endogeneity issues are common in studies in which events occur simultaneously. For example, an ad-hoc example similar to that in Armstrong, Core, and Guay's study [26] considers a research question that matters to accounting and governance: *Does financial expertise on the board affect firm disclosure?*

It is well established that the level of financial expertise on the board is a choice and is non-randomly assigned to firms. As a result, the risk of having OCVs is high, as is the threat of reverse causality since levels of financial expertise might be affected by the actual or expected level of firm disclosure.

In this example, we exploit a natural experiment offered by a fictional change in regulatory requirements (LAW) that requires that all firms have at least 50 % of

---

[8]The *Hausman test* is employed in many contexts to compare the magnitude and significance of a series of coefficients. The Hausman test is discussed in Chap. 6 to compare the results of fixed-effects and random-effects model estimation.

[9]The econometrics literature offers rich guidance in terms of the F-test values that should be used as a benchmark: If the number of *instruments* is 1, 2, or more than 5, the corresponding lower threshold of F-values are 8.96, 11.59, or higher than 15 to rule out the risk of a weak instrument.

Table 7.5 Financial expertise: descriptive statistics

Variable	Mean	Std. dev.	Min	Max
mef_ch	3.48	2.45	0.10	11
fin_exp_t1	0.68	0.15	0.50	1
fin_exp_t0	0.41	0.22	0	1
chg_fin_exp	0.27	0.24	−0.15	0.70
pred_chg_fin_exp	0.14	0.15	0	0.50
headquarters	0.54	0.50	0	1
bus_school	0.56	0.50	0	1
gco	0.32	0.47	0	1
owners_5pct	5.16	2.73	1	14
audit_fees	485.10	307.03	10	1300

Mef_ch is the difference between the average number of MEFs issued before and after LAW. *Fin_exp_t1 (Fin_exp_t0)* is the percent of financial experts on the board after (before) LAW was passed. *Pred_chg_fin_exp* is the predicted level of change in financial experts on the board required to meet the 50 % threshold. *Headquarters* is an indicator variable: a firm's headquarters is in a state capital (1) or not (0). *bus_school* is an indicator variable to proxy whether a business school is within 100 kilometers of a company's headquarters (1) or not (0). *GCO* indicates whether a company was subject to external auditors' issuing a going-concern opinion (1) or not (0) in the last 5 years. *Owners_5pct* is the number of owners with at least 5 % stake in the equity. *Audit_fees* is the amount of audit fees (in $) paid to external auditor

directors with financial expertise from time T1 onwards. Some firms are already compliant with the regulation, while others must adapt: Firms with less than 50 % of financial experts on their boards prior to T0 *must* change their board composition in order to be compliant, while firms that already meet the requirement will not adjust. Table 7.5 shows sample data.

Mef_ch is the dependent variable. The average value of *Fin_exp_t0* is smaller than the value of *Fin_exp_t1* and the variability is higher. Given that changes in board composition depend on a firm/board's voluntary choices, the variable is endogenous. Therefore, we employ *Pred_chg_fin_exp* to indicate the predicted level of change in financial experts on the board required to meet the 50 % threshold. (For example, a board that is 22 % financial experts prior to t0 has a predicted value of change of 28 %). This is a good candidate for an *instrument* because it correlates with the actual change and does not correlate with the dependent variable. The predicted change is exogenous because it stems from regulation, so it is out of the firm's direct control.

The two variables *Headquarters* and *bus_school* proxy for the availability of directors with financial expertise. *GCO* proxies for the financial viability of the business, and the literature suggests it is jointly correlated with board composition and firm disclosures. *Audit_fees* proxies for the level of effort and insurance a company buys outside; higher audit fees should indicate superior transparency.

Table 7.6 Financial expertise: breakdown by compliance

	Change sample		Compliant sample		
	Mean	Std. err.	Mean	Std. err.	t-test
mef_ch	4.30	0.41	1.55	0.29	**−4.21**
fin_exp_t1	0.66	0.02	0.70	0.03	0.62
fin_exp_t0	0.30	0.02	0.68	0.03	**8.64**
chg_fin_exp	0.37	0.03	0.02	0.02	**−6.55**
pred_chg_fin_exp	0.20	0.02	0.00	0.00	**−5.73**
headquarters	0.51	0.09	0.60	0.13	0.54
bus_school	0.57	0.08	0.53	0.13	−0.24
gco	0.34	0.08	0.27	0.12	−0.52
owners_5pct	5.48	0.48	4.40	0.62	−1.20
audit_fees	557.00	52.65	317.00	58.34	**−2.69**

Mef_ch is the difference between the average number of MEFs issued before and after LAW. *Fin_exp_t1 (Fin_exp_t0)* is the percent of financial experts on the board after (before) LAW was passed. *Pred_chg_fin_exp* is the predicted level of change in financial experts on the board required to meet the 50 % threshold. *Headquarters* is an indicator variable: a firm's headquarters is in a state capital (1) or not (0). *bus_school* is an indicator variable to proxy whether a business school is within 100 kilometers of a company's headquarters (1) or not (0). *GCO* indicates whether a company was subject to external auditors' issuing a going-concern opinion (1) or not (0) in the last 5 years. *Owners_5pct* is the number of owners with at least 5 % stake in the equity. *Audit_fees* is the amount of audit fees (in $) paid to external auditor

Table 7.6 shows the differences between the two sub-samples of firms—those that were compliant with the regulation and those that were not. The sub-samples differ in terms of financial expertise prior to the regulation (68 % vs. 30 %, respectively) of board members who were financial experts in the two sub-samples. While firms in the *compliant sample* were not expected to change their level of financial expertise—any change would be voluntary, and the predicted change in financial expertise is 0—those in the *non-compliant sample* were expected to change their level of financial expertise. Firms also differ in their disclosure behaviors (*mef_ch*), as compliant firms did not alter their policies after the regulation as much as firms that were *forced to change* board composition did (1.55 vs. 4.30, respectively).

Addressing the research question of interest through OLS estimation leads to estimating the model in Eq. (7.7).

$$\text{MEF\_ch}_i = \beta_0 + \beta_1 Chg\_fin\_exp_i + \Sigma COV + \varepsilon_i \qquad (7.7)$$

Changes in levels of financial expertise are usually endogenous, as it is a firm choice rather than the result of random assignment. Iterations between theory and data help us to identify possible remedies to endogeneity issues posited with the model. IVE requires identifying one or more *instruments* that carve out the exogenous portion of *Chg_fin_exp* to be used in the subsequent estimation of *Mef_ch*. A correlation matrix is a necessary and useful first stopping point (Table 7.7).

The correlation matrix in Table 7.7 offers important insights into the specifications of the first- and second-stage regression models. First, the outcome

Table 7.7 Financial expertise—correlation matrix

	mef_ch	fin_exp_t1	fin_exp_t0	chg_fin_exp	pred_chg_fin_exp	Head-quarter	Bus_school	gco	owners_5pct
fin_exp_t1	-0.03								
	0.81								
fin_exp_t0	**-0.62**	**0.25**							
	0.00	0.08							
chg_fin_exp	**0.57**	**0.39**	**-0.80**						
	0.00	0.01	0.00						
pred_chg_fin_exp	**0.59**	-0.16	**-0.90**	**0.76**					
	0.00	0.26	0.00	0.00					
Headquarters	0.13	0.21	-0.11	0.24	0.18				
	0.36	0.13	0.45	0.10	0.22				
bus_school	-0.02	**0.39**	-0.03	**0.28**	0.11	0.07			
	0.89	0.00	0.82	0.05	0.47	0.62			
Gco	0.23	0.01	**-0.25**	0.24	**0.33**	-0.06	-0.08		
	0.10	0.94	0.08	0.09	0.02	0.70	0.57		
owners_5pct	**0.55**	-0.18	-0.24	0.12	0.16	0.05	-0.11	-0.04	
	0.00	0.22	0.09	0.41	0.27	0.71	0.44	0.78	
audit_fees	**0.76**	-0.21	**-0.38**	0.23	**0.31**	0.06	-0.19	0.14	**0.60**
	0.00	0.15	0.01	0.10	0.03	0.67	0.19	0.33	0.00

Mef_ch is the difference between the average number of MEFs issued before and after LAW. *Fin_exp_t1* (*Fin_exp_t0*) is the percent of financial experts on the board after (before) LAW was passed. *Pred_chg_fin_exp* is the predicted level of change in financial experts on the board required to meet the 50 % threshold. *Headquarters* is an indicator variable: a firm's headquarters is within 100 km of a company's headquarters (1) or not (0). *bus_school* is an indicator variable to proxy whether a business school is in a state capital (1) or not (0). *GCO* indicates whether a company was subject to external auditors' issuing a going-concern opinion (1) or not (0) in the last 5 years. *Owners_5pct* is the number of owners with at least 5 % stake in the equity. *Audit_fees* is the amount of audit fees (in \$) paid to external auditor variable *mef_ch* is positively and significantly correlated with the main predictor *chg_fin_exp* (.57; $p < 0.001$), which makes performing additional analyses worthwhile. *Mef_ch* also correlates with *owners_5pct* (.55; $p < 0.001$) and *audit_fees* (.76; $p < 0.001$), so these variables should be added as covariates since they improve the estimation of the dependent variable.

As expected, the main predictor, *chg_fin_exp*, negatively correlates with the level of financial expertise prior to the new regulation (-0.80; $p < 0.001$). In fact, changes to board composition are larger at lower levels of financial expertise prior to T0. *chg_fin_exp* has a large and significant correlation with *bus_school* (.28; $p < 0.05$) and a less significant correlation with *gco* (.24; $p < 0.10$) and with *headquarters* (.24; $p < 0.10$). There is a high correlation between the main predictor and *pred_chg_fin_exp* (.76; $p < 0.001$), which provides some confidence in terms of the suitability of the *instrument* to be used in the IVE approach.

The first step in IVE estimation and 2SLS is defining the *first-stage regression*. A prediction model for the main (endogenous) predictor is shown in (Eq. 7.8: first-stage regression).

First-stage regression:

$$\text{Chg\_fin\_exp}_i = \alpha_0 + \alpha_1 \text{Instrument}_i + \Sigma \text{Exclusion Restrictions} + \delta_i \quad (7.8)$$

The key issue in (Eq. 7.8: first-stage regression) is identifying the *instrument* and *exclusion restrictions* (i.e., variables to be included in the *first stage* but excluded from the *second stage*). Theory and the correlation matrix suggest a number of possible routes: First, *headquarters* and *bus_school* are two variables that prior studies–and the correlation analysis to some extent–indicate as predictors of *ch_fin_exp*. Second, *pred_chg_fin_exp* appears to be a valid instrument because of its strong correlation with the main predictor; it is difficult to argue that *pred_chg_fin_exp* is endogenous given that the change has been imposed by a regulatory innovation.

Table 7.8 presents three alternative and equally plausible (ex-ante) *first-stage regression models*. All three models include the common covariates (*gco*, *audit_fees*, and *owners_5pct*) [1]. A cursory inspection of Model 1, which relies on *headquarters* and *bus_school* as the two sole predictors of *chg_fin_exp*, reveals that it has limited explanatory power (Adj-$R^2 = 8\%$) and that both the F-statistic (3.34; $p < 0.05$) and *Wald* test (0.44; $p > 0.1$) indicate low predictive ability. Weak instruments or just identified models render IVE approaches even more likely to be biased than OLS estimations do. In Model 2, *pred_chg_fin_exp* is added as the only instrument; no other covariates augment the model [27]. To determine which model is superior in terms of predictive ability we can use the Wald test to compare the model statistics and the severity of under-identification [14]. In our example, Model 2 has a much better fit with the data (Adj-$R^2 = 56\%$); both the *Wald* test (25.42; $p < 0.001$) and the F-statistic (65.01; $p < 0.001$) suggest rejecting the null hypothesis) of a weak instrument. Last, Model 3 includes all three instruments and appears to be robust enough to allow an accurate prediction (Adj-$R^2 = 60\%$); both the *Wald*

Table 7.8 Financial expertise—instrumental variables in first-stage regression

First-stage regression						
	Model 1		Model 2		Model 3	
DV: Chg_fin_exp	Coeff (se)	t	Coeff (se)	t	Coeff (se)	t
Exclusion restrictions						
headquarters	0.10 (0.069)	1.61			0.45 (0.43)	1.06
bus_school	0.12 (0.064)	1.91			0.09 (0.042)	2.12
pred_chg_fin_exp			1.16 (0.14)	8.06	1.11 (0.14)	7.81
Intercept	0.14 (0.057)	2.48	0.10 (0.03)	3.39	0.03 (0.04)	0.85
Common covariates	Included		Included		Included	
Adj-R^2	0.08		0.56		0.60	
F-test (prob)	3.34 ($p < 0.05$)		65.01 ($p < .001$)		25.39 ($p < 0.001$)	
Wald F-test	0.44 ($p > 0.05$)		25.41 ($p < 0.001$)		8.40 ($p < 0.001$)	

test (8.40; $p < 0.001$) and the F-statistic (25.39; $p < 0.001$) suggest rejecting the null hypothesis of a weak instrument.

As a result of our assessment of the potential *instrument* and *exclusion restrictions*, the first-stage regression is shown in (Eq. 7.9: first-stage regression).

First-stage regression:

$$
\begin{aligned}
\text{Chg\_fin\_exp}_i = {} & \alpha_0 + \alpha_1 \text{Pred\_chg\_fin\_exp} + \alpha_2 \text{Headquarter} \\
& + \alpha_3 \text{bus\_school} + \alpha_4 \text{gco} + \alpha_5 \text{owners\_5pct} \\
& + \alpha_6 \text{audit\_fees} + \delta_i
\end{aligned}
\tag{7.9}
$$

The next step involves estimating a *second-stage regression* by employing the fitted values of the main predictor $\hat{X}$ to assess the effects of financial expertise on firm disclosure. The second stage includes covariates to improve model estimation: In this case, both the extant literature and the correlation matrix indicate that *gco*, *audit fees*, and *owners_5pct* should be included in the model, as shown in (Eq. 7.10: second-stage regression).

Second-stage regression:

$$
\begin{aligned}
\text{Mef\_ch}_i = {} & \beta_0 + \beta_1 \widehat{\text{Chg\_fin\_exp}} + \beta_2 \text{GCO}_i + \beta_3 \text{Owners\_5pct} \\
& + \beta_4 \text{Audit\_fees} + \mu_i
\end{aligned}
\tag{7.10}
$$

The two models in (Eq. 7.9: first-stage regression) and (Eq. 7.10: second-stage regression) are estimated through a 2SLS approach.[10]

Prior to moving to the estimation results, it is worth exploring the nature of the variables:

---

[10]Statistical software (e.g. STATA, R, SAS) offers convenient routines with which to estimate 2SLS models.

1. *Endogenous predictor* (first stage only)—The endogenous predictor is the main predictor in the model (X, *chg_fin_exp*) and is subject to endogeneity issues.
2. *Instrumental variable* (first stage only)—*pred_chg_fin_exp* is the instrument identified. It correlates with the main predictor, but we can rule out endogeneity concerns because predicted change in financial expertise on the board is the result of a *natural experiment* (e.g., a change in regulations), so it is substantially independent of any firm choice.
3. *Exclusion restrictions* (first stage only)—Exclusion restrictions refer to two variables, *Headquarters* and *Bus_school*, that are included in the first-stage regression but not in the second-stage regression. Similar to the *instrument*, we must justify the exclusion (e.g., the variables do not correlate with the error term in the main model) because of IVE models' sensitivity to the specifications of the first-stage regression [14, 21].
4. *Control variables* (first- and second-stage models)—Control variables (*gco*, *owners_5pct*, and *audit fees*) are added to the second stage because they increase the estimation model's predictive ability, but they should be added to the first-stage regression as well, as failing to do so may raise concerns about the correlation with the first-stage model.
5. *Outcome* (second stage only)—M*ef_ch* is the initial dependent variable estimated in the second stage.

Table 7.9 illustrates the results of the 2SLS model, in which we specify the first- and second-stage regressions. Table 7.9 also lists the tests required when employing an IVE approach via 2SLS and a comparison of the 2SLS model with the *traditional* OLS regression in order to determine whether using IVE is warranted. Results from the *first-stage regression* indicate that the instrument *pred_chg_fin_exp* positively correlates with *chg_fin_exp* (the main predictor), as the estimation coefficient is positive and statistically significant (1.07; $p < 0.001$). This result meets one condition required to employ an IVE approach. Next, the *exclusion restrictions* are associated with the main predictor but to a lesser extent. Last, the control variables (*gco*, *owners_5pct*, and *audit_fees*) included in both the first and second stages do not display significant associations with the endogenous regressor.

The results summarize a series of diagnostic tests that assess the validity and suitability of the *instrument* and the overall *first-stage regression* in the context of a 2SLS. The results are somewhat in line with those presented in Table 7.8: The *F*-statistic (20.20; $p < 0.001$) exceeds the suggested threshold and rules out the hypothesis of *weak instruments*. Similarly, the *under-identification test* (Anderson's LM) rejects the null hypothesis)that relevant variables have been omitted from the first stage ($\chi^2 = 29.25$; $p < 0.001$). A third diagnostic test relates to the *over-identification test* (Sargan's test or Hansen's J); in this case, the concern is that too many instruments have been included in the first stage and there is a risk of redundancy. (For example, some of the variables are not needed and may correlate with the error term in the outcome model.) Sargan's test indicates that we fail to reject the null hypothesis)that *instruments are not redundant* ($\chi^2 = .396$; $p = 0.82$).

Table 7.9 Financial expertise: comparison of OLS and the IVE approach

	OLS		IV & 2SLS estimation			
			First stage		*Second stage*	
	Coeff (se)	t	Coeff (se)	t	Coeff (se)	z
Chg_fin_exp	4.15 (0.79)	5.23			5.03 (0.99)	5.04
First-stage Instruments						
headquarters			0.46 (0.044)	1.04		
business_school			0.097 (0.045)	2.13		
pred_chg_fin_exp			1.07 (0.16)	6.50		
Controls						
gco	0.34 (0.39)	0.86	0.012 (0.05)	0.25	0.24 (0.38)	0.64
owners_5pct	0.159 (0.082)	1.94	−0.01 (0.001)	−0.03	0.15 (0.078)	2.01
adit_fees	0.004 (0.001)	5.96	0.001 (0.001)	0.40	0.004 (0.001)	5.96
Intercept	−0.71 (0.42)	−1.68	0.014 (0.063)	0.23	−0.85 (0.42)	−2.02
Diagnostic Tests						
Adj-R2	0.74		0.72			
F-test: H0: Instruments are weak.			20.20 ($p < 0.001$)			
Under-identification test (Anderson's LM)—H0: Instruments have been excluded.			29.25 ($p < 0.001$)			
Over-identification test (Sargan's test)—H0: Instruments are not redundant.			0.396 ($p = 0.82$)			
Wu-Hausman test—H0: endogenous regressors			1.95 ($p = 0.167$)			
VIFs (max)	1.67					

In addition to testing the suitability of the *first stage*, an important additional diagnostic is the *Wu-Hausman test* for endogeneity, which compares the IVE and OLS coefficients to determine whether they differ. If they are close, then there is no evidence with which to reject the null hypothesis. Here, the test fails to reject the hypothesis that OLS estimation is endogenous compared to the IVE (1.96; $p = .167$), thus casting doubt on the need to employ a more costly and sensitive estimation model if the advantages are not clear.

Once we have ascertained that the *instrument* is valid and the *exclusion restrictions* are justified, we can turn to the results of the second-stage regression. Overall, there is clear evidence that increases in the board's financial expertise positively affect the disclosure policies and firm transparency, measured as the change in the number of management earnings forecasts released (5.03; $z < 0.001$). Given that we can maintain the hypothesis of the *instrument's* exogeneity, we can offer a causal interpretation to the coefficient: an increase in level of financial expertise on the board improves a firm's disclosure and overall transparency.

Finally, in order to address concerns related to endogeneity, we report results from an OLS estimation, where the main predictor is *chg_fin_exp*, labeled as endogenous in the first instance. OLS regression reports similar results for the second-stage regression model: the coefficient on *chg_fin_exp* is still positive and highly significant, although it is smaller than its instrumented version (4.15; $p < 0.001$).

In spite of the striking similarity of the results offered by OLS regression and IVE-2SLS, convincing *instruments* and a defensible *first-stage regression* will attenuate the endogeneity concerns. If all the stringent conditions to ensuring valid IVE and 2SLS estimations are met, then these approaches should be preferred over an OLS approach. Nevertheless, presenting results from OLS regression will allow a more direct comparison and assessment of the IVE estimation, given that these estimations are highly sensitive to alternative specifications.

Addressing Self-Selection: The Inverse Mills Ratio or Heckman Selection Procedure

The Inverse Mills Ratio (IMR) or Heckman selection procedure [28] is a technique with which to address *selection bias* that is due to "unobservables" by estimating a bias correction term (the Inverse Mills Ratio) that augments the number of parameters in the second-stage regression model. The coefficient estimate offers guidance in terms of the sign and extent of the bias. The IMR approach is employed in two types of potential endogeneity concerns [14]:

1. *Treatment effect model*: The main predictor (X) is an endogenous dummy variable (e.g., the decision to hire a Big-4 Audit Firm, to employ a more complex costing model, to issue an IPO). In this case, the value of the treatment (1 or 0) depends on whether the units choose to do something, as the drivers of their choice may affect the outcome variable as well.
2. *Sample selection model*: The selection issue arises because the values of the outcome variable (Y) are available only for a subset of observations. For example, a researcher who wishes to explore the determinants of audit fees for Big-4 auditors or the IPO premium for companies that go public would face a condition in which the outcome variable is not available for all observations but only for those units that hire a Big-4 auditor or choose to go public. In this case, the potential for endogeneity arises as a consequence of the choice to hire or not hire a Big-4 auditor or the choice to go public or stay private.

The implementation of the Heckman selection procedure follows the same steps in both cases and allows similar interpretations of the regression models involved.

Generally speaking, an IMR procedure is employed when we are trying to estimate the outcome model shown in (Eq. 7.11: outcome model).

Outcome model:

$$Y_i = \alpha_0 + \alpha_1 D_i + \Sigma\alpha COV + \varepsilon_i \qquad (7.11)$$

In (Eq. 7.11: outcome model), Y is the outcome variable, D is a *choice* variable that takes the value of 1 or 0, and COV represents a set of covariates that should be included in the estimation model either because they will improve the overall model fit or because of the potential for OCVs. (See section 5.3.) Given that D is endogenous, a *first-stage regression* in the form of a *probit* model is specified as shown in (Eq. 7.12: first-stage regression).

First-stage regression:

$$D_i = \beta_0 + \beta_1 Z_1 + \beta_n Z_n + u_i \qquad (7.12)$$

In (Eq. 7.12: first-stage regression), D is the treatment variable in the original model and $Z_1 \ldots Z_n$ represent a set of *exclusion variables* that are employed in the estimation of D but that will be excluded from the estimation of Y. The *exclusion restrictions* must not be correlated with the outcome variable (Y). From the first-stage regression, we estimate for each unit the values of IMR, which indicates the likelihood that units will get the treatment (D = 1 or D = 0). Then, by plugging IMR into the second-stage regression model, we test whether IMR affects the outcome variable. Then the sign and significance of the coefficient on the IMR in the second stage will reveal the extent of the bias on the main predictor in the outcome model.

The dependent variable in the original model (Y) is then estimated in a *second-stage regression* that is similar to the *outcome model*, with the notable exception of including the IMR coefficient that returns the extent of the bias. Hence:

Second-stage regression:

$$Y_i = \alpha_0 + \alpha_1 D_i + \Sigma COV + \alpha_2 IMR + \varepsilon_i \qquad (7.13)$$

As for the set of exclusion restrictions–the so-called Z variables–added in the first stage model, they must be exogenous; otherwise the regression coefficients in the first stage will be biased. In addition, the reasons for the exclusion of the Z variables from the second-stage regression must be economically valid and justified such that theory does not suggest any correlation between Z and Y. Overall, the main challenge to the successful application of the IMR (Heckman selection test) lies in identifying good Z variables.

To illustrate the application of the IMR estimation, consider an example that follows the empirical tests proposed by Lennox et al. [14]. The example illustrates the logic and the technical issues related to the application of the IMR approach. The empirical question of interest concerns whether *firms that engage in a seasoned equity offering (SEO) experience an increase or a decrease in audit fees.* The economic rationale that underlies this question leads to either a potentially positive

Table 7.10 SEO and
audit fees: descriptives

Variable	Mean	Std. dev.	Min	Max
DV_FEES	216	97.75	50	540
SEO	1	0.51	0	1
gco	0	0.49	0	1
size_asset	2852	2046.38	120	8543
age	67	34.62	8.40	180
ROA	0.14	0.08	0.01	0.45

DV_Fees, the outcome variable, expresses the annual fees paid to
the auditor. *SEO*, the main predictor, is a dummy variable that
indicates whether a company has issued an SEO (1) or not (0).
GCO is a dummy variable that indicates whether the external
auditor has issued a GCO (1) or not (0). *Size_asset* proxies for
size, measured in terms of dollar amount of assets. *Age* indicates
the number of years the company has been listed on the stock
exchange. *ROA* is a profitability measure in the form of a ratio of
return on assets

relationship (e.g., auditors incur more complexity and auditing costs) or a negative
relationship (e.g., raising additional equity capital strengthens the company and
reduces financial risk, as both factors are priced into audit-fee models). Let us
assume the collected data looks as Table 7.10 shows.

SEO, as the main predictor, requires more attention. Choosing to issue additional
equity on the financial market is voluntary and may depend on other factors that
jointly affect the outcome variable (*audit fees*), so there is a threat of endogeneity
that should be taken into account. The literature suggests that a number of variables
can affect the relationship of interest, some of which are observable (e.g., firm age,
size), while others (e.g., volatility) are not. Unlike the previous case (independent
board directors), the source of endogeneity comes from both observable and
unobservable factors. The outcome model we would specify is shown in
(Eq. 7.14: outcome model).

Outcome model:

$$DV\_FEES_i = \alpha_0 + \alpha_1 SEO_i + \Sigma COV + \varepsilon_i \qquad (7.14)$$

The IMR approach is well suited to assessing the extent of endogeneity bias in
the relationship of interest. The first step involves modeling a *first-stage regression*,
where the main predictor of interest (*SEO*) becomes a function of a series of Z
variables that determine the choice to raise or not raise equity capital, but they must
not be related to audit fees. The extant literature and the correlation matrix are two
tools that can guide the specification of the *first-stage regression*. The correlation
matrix is particularly useful, as shown in Table 7.11.

Table 7.11 shows the positive and significant coefficient between *DV_Fees* and
SEO, suggesting an increase in audit fees in the case of SEO. The correlation matrix
also suggests that both *age* and *size_asset* are predictors of *SEO* but are uncorrelated
with the dependent variable of interest. Hence, these are two candidates to be the
exclusion restrictions in a first-stage model. In a similar fashion, Table 7.11 shows

Table 7.11 SEO and audit fees: correlation matrix

	DV_FEES	SEO	Age	size_asset	GCO
SEO	0.27				
	0.06				
age	0.00	0.34			
	0.97	0.02			
size_asset	0.08	0.28	−0.14		
	0.56	0.05	0.32		
gco	0.26	−0.16	0.09	−0.18	
	0.07	0.26	0.51	0.20	
ROA	−0.31	0.20	0.36	−0.13	−0.17
	0.03	0.17	0.01	0.37	0.24

DV_Fees, the outcome variable, expresses the annual fees paid to the auditor. *SEO*, the main predictor, is a dummy variable that indicates whether a company has issued an SEO (1) or not (0). *GCO* is a dummy variable that indicates whether the external auditor has issued a GCO (1) or not (0). *Size_asset* proxies for size, measured in terms of dollar amount of assets. *Age* indicates the number of years the company has been listed on the stock exchange. *ROA* is a profitability measure in the form of a ratio of return on assets

that *GCO* and *ROA* are positively and negatively correlated with the *DV_Fees*, respectively, suggesting their inclusion in the second-stage model. Therefore, the two models are as shown in (Eq. 7.15: first-stage regression:).

First-stage regression:

$$SEO_i = \beta_0 + \beta_1 AGE_i + \beta_2 ASSET_i + \nu_i \qquad (7.15)$$

The first-stage regression is estimated as a probit model (Table 7.12). We need this model because it helps in assessing the model's overall predictive ability in relation to the main predictor (*SEO*) and it returns the IMR to be added to the second-stage regression.

The *first-stage model* shows a good fit (pseudo-$R^2 = 18.75$ and Log-likelihood $= -28.16$), suggesting that IMR be included in the second-stage regression, as shown in (Eq. 7.16: second-stage regression).

Second-stage regression:

$$DV\_FEES_i = \alpha_0 + \alpha_1 SEO_i + \alpha_2 ROA_i + \alpha_3 GCO_i + \alpha_4 IMR_i + \varepsilon_i \quad (7.16)$$

The second-stage regression is similar to the outcome model but with the inclusion of the *IMR* variable's indicating the extent of the bias. The *exclusion variables* (*size_asset* and *age*) are kept out of the model, whereas *ROA* and *GCO* are added to improve the estimation and accuracy of the second stage.

The results shown in Table 7.13 offer three important indications regarding our theoretical question: (1) The coefficient on *SEO* is positive and statistically significant, suggesting that firms that offer equity on the market will experience higher audit fees. (2) The coefficient on IMR is not statistically significant, indicating that the selection problem is negligible. A positive or negative and significant

Table 7.12 SEO and audit fees: first-stage regression model

First-stage model of SEO choice

	Coeff/se	Z
Size_Asset	0.00026	2.40
	0.00010	
Age	0.018	2.68
	0.006	
Intercept	−1.910	−3.12
	0.614	
Pseudo-R^2	18.75	
Log_likelihood	−28.16	

coefficient would instead suggest the existence of a potential *selection problem* that would pose issues in relation to the interpretation of the results. (3) The VIF values are small (maximum value = 1.38), suggesting that multicollinearity is not an issue in the second-stage regression.

This example shows a relatively straightforward way to employ IMR to detect the extent of the bias that is due to potential self-selection problems caused by the voluntary nature of the main predictor (e.g., to issue or not issue an SEO). Still, researchers should exercise caution in defining the *first-* and *second-stage regression models* because of the IMR approach's sensitivity to model specifications [21]. Therefore, there are several guidelines for executing and reporting the appropriate procedures:

1. Report OLS results (without IMR) to reinforce the credibility of results.
2. Define and justify a set of exclusion restrictions (the Z variables), going from *first-* to *second*-stage regressions. While it is possible to estimate a first stage without Z variables, doing so is not recommended, as it impairs the soundness of the methodology and renders interpretation more difficult.
3. Report the full model specified in the *first-stage probit model*.
4. Specify alternative models using different Z variables and compare the consistency of the results. IMR is highly sensitive to the changes in exclusion restrictions on the estimated coefficients and their interpretation.
5. Report multicollinearity (VIFs) in the second-stage regression to attenuate concerns about the presence of IMR and Z variables in the same model.

An example is shown in Table 7.14 and in Table 7.15.

Table 7.14 shows results from an OLS regression, where *DV_fees* is the dependent variable and *SEO* is the main predictor. The OLS regression offers results that are identical to those of the two-stage Heckman selection procedure, which reinforces the credibility of conclusions. Although similar to the IMR approach, the OLS regression results should be mentioned in the empirical section.

The next example shows the effects of **failing to identify** valid *exclusion restrictions* in the first model. More specifically, it presents a case in which there

Table 7.13 SEO and audit fees: second-stage regression model

Second-stage treatment model		
	Coeff (se)	T
SEO	76.61	2.74
	27.95	
ROA	−409.24	−2.42
	169.00	
GCO	51.56	2.01
	25.70	
IMR	11.95	0.29
	41.66	
Pseudo-R^2	21.15	
VIF (max)	1.38	

Table 7.14 SEO and audit fees: comparison of second-stage and OLS models

Model I Second-stage heckman model			Model II OLS regression	
	Coeff/se	t	Coeff/se	t
SEO	76.61	2.74	73.17	2.95
	27.95		25.01	
ROA	−409.24	−2.42	−423.28	−2.64
	169.00		160.22	
GCO	51.56	2.01	51.14	2.01
	25.70		25.40	
IMR	11.95	0.29		
	41.66			
Intercept			220.32	7.18
			30.69	
Observations	50		50	
Pseudo-R^2	21.15		21.15	
VIF (max)	1.38		1.06	

are no exclusion restrictions and the predictors in the *first-stage regression* (*age* and *size_asset*) are added as covariates in the *second-stage regression*.

Adding the same covariates (*age* and *size_asset*) to the second-stage regression triggers a multicollinearity (max VIFs $= 20.21$) that significantly alters the interpretability of the results. Even though the regression coefficient on *SEO* is substantially the same, one cannot securely establish whether IMR offers a valid assessment of the potential endogeneity in the model.

Examining Counterfactual Models: The Propensity Score Method

The propensity score method (PSM) is another way to address endogeneity concerns when using non-experimental, observational data [3, 24]. The issue researchers face is the lack of a *counterfactual model* for the treatment group that fulfills the "*everything else equal*" condition. The treatment (X) is non-randomly

Table 7.15 SEO and audit fees: alternative identification of Z variables

Second-stage model alternative specifications of the first stage		
	Coeff/se	T
SEO	77.33	2.66
	29.04	
ROA	−409.24	−2.26
	180.94	
GCO	49.88	1.73
	28.79	
AGE	0.16	0.11
	1.46	
Size_Asset	0.01	0.09
	0.02	
IMR	24.16	0.19
	126.50	
Pseudo-R^2	27.67	
VIF (max)	20.21	

assigned to the observed units, as it is a choice. PSM is particularly well suited for identifying good counterfactuals from observational data, as it randomizes (ex-post) units to the treatment and control conditions as would be done in an experiment. PSM employs observational data to derive good comparable groups, but if the source of selection is due to unobservable factors, its usefulness is questionable.

PSM works with the idea of matching treated with non-treated (i.e., control) units. Matching using covariates is ideal when the number of dimensions is limited and manageable. PSM returns the probability that a unit is treated, regardless of whether the unit has *actually* been treated. Each unit gets a *score* that indicates a *propensity* for being treated. In a pool of similar units in terms of their score researchers can then compare values on the outcome variable for units that have been treated with those that have not been treated.

PSM uses characteristics for which data can be gathered to estimate *propensity scores* that reflect the probability that a unit receives (or not) a treatment. This process requires a certain level of abstraction because the units either have been treated (*treated*) or not (*control*). While real choices are a reflection of endogenous characteristics, the *propensity score* is based on a number of factors that determine the choice (X). PSM's effectiveness is based on how well the observable covariates predict the scores of the units, rendering them comparable. PSM is helpful in clarifying whether the units that receive the treatment (or a level of it) are comparable across a number of dimensions (e.g., the observable covariates) to the units that do not receive it. If there is no overlap between the groups or it is not possible to identify matching firms, we would conclude that companies in the treatment and control conditions are *not identical across dimensions* that affect the outcome, so the endogeneity will result in biased estimation coefficients.

Table 7.16 Education example: descriptive statistics

Variable	Obs	Mean	Std. dev.	Min	Max
math12	5671	51.051	9.502	29.880	71.370
catholic	5671	0.104	0.306	0.0	1.0
math8	5671	51.490	9.683	34.480	77.200
faminc8	5671	9.526	2.218	1	12

Math12, the outcome variable (Y), indicates the score an individual student obtained in a standardized test of mathematics in their high school year 12. *Catholic* is the treatment (X) variable in the form of a dummy that indicates attendance (1) or not (0) in a Catholic school. Other covariates are *Math8*, the score obtained in a standardized test of mathematics in their high school year 8. Last, *faminc8* refers to the student's level of family income in year 8, from 1 (low income) to 12 (high income)

To illustrate the application of PSM estimation, we use an example from the education field: data from the National Education Longitudinal Study [29] in the US.[11] The question of interest was whether enrollment in Catholic high schools exerted a positive effect on students' achievement. Consider, for example, the data in Table 7.16 on a cohort of US high-school students.

The choice to attend or not attend a Catholic school is not random, as it depends on a series of factors that can also affect a student's achievement. Some of these factors are observable (e.g., family income and pre-admission tests), whereas others are not (e.g., a family's attitude toward religion). A starting point for answering our research question involves a two-sample *t*-test.

Results from a *t*-test reported in Table 7.17 suggest that attending a Catholic school had a positive effect on achievement for the 592 students that attended a Catholic school: The difference in the *math12* test scores is large (-3.89 for those who attended a non-Catholic school) and statistically significant. Even so, claiming causality requires that the two groups must be equal and comparable across dimensions that affect students' achievement. To determine whether such is the case, we start by inspecting a correlation matrix (Table 7.18).

The correlations reveal that *family income* (in year 8) positively and significantly correlates with both the main predictor (*catholic*) and the outcome (*math12*). *math8* also correlates with *math12* and *catholic*.

Stratification, an important feature of PSM, marks its difference from the regression approach. The two covariates that should be used to stratify the sample are *faminc8* and *math8*. Results are presented in Table 7.19.

Table 7.19 compares the scores on *math12* across students who attend and students who do not attend a Catholic high school. It shows that the positive effect of attending a Catholic school diminishes at higher levels of family income (Table 7.19: 3.76, 3.51 or 2.12). When stratifying on *math8*, the differences across levels of math proficiency do not transfer to the two categories of attending or not a

---

[11]This example is reported in Murnane and Willet [3] in much more detail. We refer the reader directly to this valuable source for an in-depth assessment and understanding of the example.

Table 7.17 Education example: univariate comparison across groups

Variable	Obs	Mean	Std. err.	Std. dev.	[95 % Conf. interval]	
no_cath	5079	50.645	0.134	9.534	50.382	50.907
yes_cath	592	54.540	0.348	8.463	53.856	55.223
Diff		−3.895	0.409			
t-test		−9.51				

Table 7.18 Education example: correlation matrix

	math12	catholic	faminc8
catholic	0.13		
	0.00		
faminc8	0.31	0.13	
	0.00	0.00	
math8	0.83	0.08	0.29
	0.00	0.00	0.00

Table 7.19 Education example: stratification

	no_cath	yes_cath	Diff	T
Stratification on income				
Low_INCOME	46.77	50.53	3.76	3.46
Mid_INCOME	50.34	53.85	3.51	4.82
High_INCOME	53.59	55.71	2.12	4.02
Stratification on Math8				
Low_Math8	36.8	36.3	−0.50	1.72
Mid_Math8	41.09	41.24	0.15	−0.82
High_Math8	47.49	47.92	0.43	−2.33
VeryHigh_Math8	60.01	59.48	−0.53	1.51

catholic school, and the Catholic school effect vanishes. (For example, scores on *math12* improve with increases in *math8* but not as a result of attending a Catholic school.) Overall, there are twelve possible groups because of the crossing of two dimensions (math at year 8 and family income) with three (*faminc8*) and four (*math8*) categories, respectively. One would not be able to achieve this result using a regression approach.

The stratification procedure (Fig. 7.5) is central to the PSM approach. PSM's attempt to identify the peers of the 592 students who attended a Catholic high school so treatment and control groups can be identified is based on a propensity score that returns the likelihood of each student's being enrolled in a Catholic school. PSM ignores whether students are actually enrolled in a Catholic school, at least in the first phase. The stratification and correlation matrix suggest that *math8* and *faminc8* are relevant because students with higher scores in *math8* and those with higher *faminc8* scores are more likely to attend a Catholic school.

PSM then allows a comparison of the twelve homogenous groups of students that are similar in terms of the likelihood of enrolling in a Catholic school. For instance, students included in the high_income and mid_math8 (or low_income and

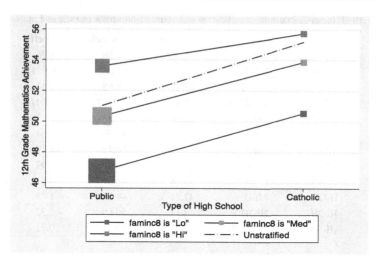

Fig. 7.5 Education example—comparison across type of school

veryHigh_math8) groups are equally likely to enroll in a Catholic school. There-fore, students in each cluster are comparable and *expected to be similar* except for whether they attend a Catholic school. The software employed to use a PSM technique estimates propensity scores in the background and associates similar units (students, in this case).

Table 7.20 reports a summary of the OLS regression coefficients and the differences in *math12* between students who attend a Catholic school and those who do not in each group. Results from clustering into twelve groups offer a different perspective from that of the *t*-test performed earlier. The differences in terms of attendance in a Catholic school are much more attenuated and seem to matter primarily at medium levels of income.

The next step involves estimation using PSM. Table 7.21 reports results from the PSM model using *psmatch2* in STATA 14. PSM involves estimating a probit regression in the first step. In doing so, we test the suitability of the covariates in predicting the treatment variable. The *probit* allows the estimation of *propensity scores* for the identification of peer observations to be matched. The pseudo-R^2 indicates the ability of the covariates in identifying proper matches. In this example, the pseudo-R^2 of 0.0319 shows a poor overall fit of the model and casts doubt on PSM's ability to identify suitable matches. Next, the average treatment estimation offers indications in two hypothetical conditions: (1) the effect of attending Catho-lic schools on the unmatched sample (e.g., students who the propensity scores indicate should not attend Catholic school but did), and (2) the effect of attending Catholic schools on the treated sample (e.g., students who the propensity scores indicate should attend Catholic school and did).

Table 7.20 Education example: stratification and comparison across income and math8 scores

Group	faminc8	math8	no_cath	yes_cath	Coeff	T
1	LOW	LOW	36.8	42.56	5.76	1.42
2	LOW	MED	40.99	41.061	0.071	0.62
3	LOW	HIGH	47.12	48.65	1.53	0.95
4	LOW	V_HIGH	56.11	56.157	0.047	0.41
5	MED	LOW	37.98	39.81	1.83	0.45
6	MED	MED	41.92	44.56	2.64	**2.52**
7	MED	HIGH	47.94	50.13	2.19	**2.57**
8	MED	V_HIGH	57.41	59.4	1.99	**2.74**
9	HIGH	LOW	39.78	40.39	0.61	0.22
10	HIGH	MED	42.74	44.22	1.48	1.49
11	HIGH	HIGH	49.17	50.69	1.52	**2.14**
12	HIGH	V_HIGH	58.93	59.65	0.72	1.59

Table 7.21 Education example, propensity-score matching

Probit regression—DV: catholic			
	Coefficient	Std. err.	z
math8	0.0077	0.0024	3.19
faminc8	0.115	0.013	8.8
intercept	−2.79	0.16	−17.1
Log likelihood	−1837.154		
Pseudo-R^2	0.0319		

Avg. treatment estimation		Treated	Control	Dif	Std. err.	t-stat
math12	unmatched	54.53	50.64	3.89	0.409	9.51
	ATT	54.53	52.87	1.66	0.54	3.07

7.5   Some Caveats and Limitations

Successful data analysis hinges on ex ante identifying and measuring all observable factors that may bias in coefficient estimates. This requirement is a study-design choice, so effort must go into data collection. The more successful this endeavor, the easier substantiating claims during data analysis will be. Issues with unobservables are even trickier to address [19].

Any empirical study that employs non-experimental and randomized data will suffer from endogeneity issues. Even so, we should not stop conducting empirical research but should explicitly address endogeneity issues and discuss how we have sought to overcome them with logical arguments and empirical tests.

Mo statistical or econometric test or specification will help us state with certainty that an estimated coefficient is unbiased and efficient. OLS, instrumental variables and 2SLS, Heckman selection models, and PSM will all return results that are subject to interpretation prior to making any claims or ruling out endogeneity concerns [30]. The ultimate test should be conducted in close connection with economic theory and should compare the variables and models to be specified.[12]

References

1. Angrist JD, Pischke JS (2008) Mostly harmless econometrics: an empiricist's companion. Princeton University Press, Princeton, NJ
2. Iyengar RJ, Zampelli EM (2009) Self-selection, endogeneity, and the relationship between CEO duality and firm performance. Strategic Manage J 30:1092–1112
3. Murnane R, Willett J (2010) Methods matter. Oxford University Press, Oxford
4. Runkel P, McGrath JE (1972) Research on human behavior: a systematic guide to method. Holt, Rinehart and Winston, New York
5. Wooldridge JM (2009) Introductory econometrics: a modern approach. South-Western Cengage Learning, Mason, OH
6. Libby R, Bloomfield R, Nelson MW (2002) Experimental research in financial accounting. Account Org Soc 27(8):775–810
7. Gassen J (2014) Causal inference in empirical archival financial accounting research. Account Org Soc 39(7):535–544
8. Morgan SL, Winship C (2007) Counterfactuals and causal analysis: methods and principles for social research. Cambridge University Press, New York
9. Rosenbaum PR, Rubin DB (1985) Constructing a control group using multivariate matched sampling methods that incorporate the propensity score. Am Stat 39(1):33–38
10. Certo ST, Busenbark JR, Woo H-S, Semadeni M (2016) Sample selection bias and Heckman models in strategic management research. Strategic Manage J. doi:10.1002/smj.2475
11. Semadeni M, Withers MC, Certo ST (2014) The perils of endogeneity and instrumental variables in strategic research: understanding through simulations. Strategic Manage J 35 (7):1070–1079
12. Kennedy P (2003) A guide to econometrics. MIT Press, Cambridge, MA
13. Maddala G (1991) A perspective on the use of limited-dependent and qualitative variables models in accounting research. Account Rev 66(4):788–807
14. Lennox CS, Francis JR, Wang Z (2011) Selection models in accounting research. Account Rev 87(2):589–616
15. Larcker DF, Rusticus TO (2007) Endogeneity and empirical accounting research. Eur Account Rev 16(1):207–215
16. Chenhall RH, Moers F (2007) The issue of endogeneity within theory-based, quantitative management accounting research. Eur Account Rev 16(1):173–196
17. Schroeder DA (2010) Accounting and causal effects. Econometric challenges 5. Springer Science & Business Media, Berlin
18. Antonakis J, Bendahan S, Jacquart P, Lalive R (2010) On making causal claims: a review and recommendations. Leadersh Q 21:1086–1120
19. Roberts MR, Whited TM (2013) Endogeneity in empirical corporate finance, Handbook of the economics of finance. Elsevier, Amsterdam, pp 493–572

---

[12]All of the issues raised in this chapter follow in the realm of a frequentist parametric framework. Other methods, including non-parametric methods, have been employed to minimize the potential issues with self-selection that are due to unobservables. For instance, Bayesian approaches have been suggested to evaluate treatment effects when selections are based on unobservables. A note of caution is required, given the limited applications of such an approach in the accounting (and finance) literature and because of the lack of evidence on the advantages of this approach over a frequentist approach.

20. Larcker DF, Rusticus TO (2010) On the use of instrumental variables in accounting research. J Account Econ 49(3):186–205
21. Tucker JW (2010) Selection bias and econometric remedies in accounting and finance research. J Account Lit 29:31–57
22. Hamilton BH, Nickerson JA (2003) Correcting for endogeneity in strategic management research. Strategic Org 1:51–78
23. Bascle G (2008) Controlling for endogeneity with instrumental variables in strategic management research. Strategic Org 6:285–327
24. Li M (2013) Using the propensity score method to estimate causal effects: a review and practical guide. Org Res Methods 16:188–226
25. Gippel J, Smith T, Zhu Y (2015) Endogeneity in accounting and finance research: natural experiments as a state-of-the-art solution. Abacus 51(2):143–168
26. Armstrong CS, Core JE, Guay WR (2014) Do independent directors cause improvements in firm transparency? J Financ Econ 113:383–403
27. Lennox CS, Wu X, Zhang T (2014) Does mandatory rotation of audit partners improve audit quality? Account Rev 89(5):1775–1803
28. Heckman J (1979) Sample selection bias as a specification error. Econometrica 47(1):53–161
29. National Education Longitudinal Study 1988. https://nces.ed.gov/surveys/nels88/index.asp
30. Gow ID, Larcker DF, Reiss PC (2015) Causal inference in accounting research. Working Paper

How to Start Analyzing, Test Assumptions and Deal with that Pesky *p*-Value

This chapter discusses the steps to take before any of the analyses discussed in earlier chapters. Although it may seem counterintuitive to put this information at the end of this book, experience teaches us that these are things people do not want to read first when they embark on their analysis journey. We all start out with a big idea and full of courage, but all too often our courage is blown to bits because words and terms like "homoscedasticity," "skewness," and "multivariate normality" make our heads spin and our plans seem impossible. However, we hope that, after you have gotten a kick from seeing first results with the method of your choice, you are now ready to learn about all the things you should have done first—the things that make your results credible.

No data is perfect, but understanding how imperfect your data is, correcting the most important imperfections, or using a different method will help you to obtain credible results from your imperfect data. The first step on the journey is to **structure** your data in a way that best fits your research questions and analysis plan. Then some thorough **cleaning** will rid your data of imperfections in the details before you start to understand the larger imperfections. These larger imperfections and the relationships in your data are first explored by **summarizing and visualizing data**. These are the topics of Sect. 7.1.

After that, we have a more thorough look at the possible larger imperfections by discussing how to test the important **assumptions** with which your data must align. The four groups of assumptions we discuss are independence, normality, homogeneity of variance, and linearity. We discuss how to test whether these assumptions hold for your data and briefly introduce strategies for when they do not.

Finally, we share some of the latest thinking and our perspective on **how to deal with that pesky *p*-value**. This issue of the correct use of the *p*-statistics is prevalent and ubiquitous, and you are well served to follow the debate and stay current in this regard.

© Springer International Publishing Switzerland 2017
W. Mertens et al., *Quantitative Data Analysis*, DOI 10.1007/978-3-319-42700-3_8

8.1   Structuring, Cleaning, and Summarizing Data

As we mentioned in the introduction to this book, analyzing data typically starts with a phase of structuring, cleaning, and exploring. You could call this process "sensemaking" of the data—working to understand what you have. Extracting meaning from data requires it to be structured in a logical and consistent way and ridding it of unreliable and invalid data. Once that is done, we can start exploring and summarizing the data in statistics and graphs. Let's discuss each of these steps in turn.

8.1.1   Structuring Data

Step 1: Structure Cases in Accordance with Your Research Question(s) The first step is to structure data in a format that allows you to run analyses easily and that allows you to answer your research question(s). Most people do not realize at first that surveys, experiments, and other kinds of data do not usually emerge in the kind of organized structure we need to run our analyses.

The best structure for most statistical programs to operate well is to have one row for each unique case and one column for each variable. In the social sciences, a case is typically constituted of a person, a team, a business unit, or an organization—whichever is the smallest relevant unit of analysis. Therefore, the case should be at the level at which you measure your most detailed variable unless it makes your data more detailed than necessary to answer your research question. For example, if you want to investigate the effect of introducing a new IT tool by comparing branches of a retail organization (e.g., some with and some without the tool), the unit of analysis is the branch. Structuring data at the employee level would make the data complex and would not contribute to answering your research question. If you measure variables at both the individual and the team level, a row typically represents one person, the smallest unit of analysis. Persons who are members of the same team will have the same values for variables measured at the team level. However, if you are interested only in team-level dynamics, you may want to aggregate individual data so you have one value for each variable for each team. If one person or team has multiple values for one variable, such as when that variable is measured multiple times, each of these values will be captured in a separate column (and, thus, act as a separate variable). Table 8.1 illustrates this structure.

Structuring data this way usually solves the confusion surrounding *nested* data—that is, "data within data" or multilevel data. For the example illustrated in Table 8.1, we could say that the variable "role" is nested in the variable "case ID," and "case ID" is nested in the variable "team size": one person can have multiple roles, and one team can have multiple persons. (Refer to Chaps. 5 and 6 to learn more about nestedness.) In that sense, it could appear that "role" is the smallest possible identifier; but if we use "role" as the identifier, we would have more persons nested within each role than we have roles nested within persons.

Table 8.1 Example of structured data

Case ID	Age	Role 1	Role 2	Team	Team size
Person 1	27	Lecturer	Ethics advisor	1	19
Person 2	43	Professor	Head of School	1	19
Person 3	37	Lecturer	Tutor	2	12
...	...	...	...	...	...

Variables that are uniquely related to one person could also be nested within "role" (e.g., all professors are older and have a bigger team to care for), which would increase the complexity of the data structure and interpretation. We would consider such a data structure only if our research questions required analysis at the level of roles, rather than persons, illustrating again that the case is as much a theoretical choice as an empirical characteristic of the data.

Step 2: Structure Variables in Accordance with Your Research Question In the next step in structuring data, nominal or categorical variables that have a limited set of values are typically re-coded from words to numbers to ease their use in analyses—for example, as a grouping variable in ANOVA. For example, female and male become 1 and 2, or we identify the reference category (e.g., female) and "no" and "yes" become 0 and 1. Make sure to take notes of how values were recoded (e.g., by assigning labels in the data set)! *Do not assume you will remember*; you may want to reuse data or have to come back to your data months or even years after you first structured it.[1]

A final step in structuring data consists of combining multiple variables into one and/or deleting variables that are unnecessary for the analyses. Although it is important to keep a version of the raw and complete dataset, most data sets have variables that are irrelevant to a particular focus and variables that are fragmented (e.g., when one of five boxes had to be ticked, resulting in five yes-no binary variables). Ensuring that the data has enough information and detail for the analyses, and no extraneous data, will save a lot of time.

8.1.2 Cleaning Data

Cleaning data means deleting *invalid* cases and dealing with *unreliable* data. **Invalid cases** are cases that do not reflect the population you are studying. For example, if you are studying small businesses and you define them as businesses with 5–50 employees, businesses with 51 or 2 employees are invalid cases. If you are studying lecturers, students are invalid cases. In short, invalid cases are cases that should not be part of your sample. The easiest way to spot them is to study

---

[1]As an example, software like STATA and SAS allow you to use text (or do-files, in STATA terms) to record the steps taken to clean the data and run the analyses.

frequencies and other descriptives of demographic data, armed with an understanding of what a valid case looks like in your situation.

Unreliable Data is data in which the values obtained for certain variables do not represent the actual values. In other words, there is nothing wrong with having the case in the data, but the values recorded for the case do not reflect the real properties of that case. An example is a reported age of 174, as it is currently impossible that this is anyone's real age. Cases often have multiple unreliable values, at which time such a case becomes unreliable as a whole.

Five characteristics of your data that can help you to spot and deal with these unreliable cases are missing data, inconsistent data, improbable response times, extreme tendencies, and extreme scores or cases (i.e., outliers). We next discuss strategies for finding and dealing with each of these, along with z-scores and normal distributions, but first, a word of warning: Cleaning data requires dealing with unreliable data and invalid cases, not deleting *inconvenient* cases. It is easy to get so passionate about your hypotheses that you unintentionally start influencing the data. Cases should be excluded only as a last resort, and doing so should not affect the direction or significance of your results but should increase their credibility. Credibility is derived in part from your study's statistical power, which depends in part on a sufficient number of cases in your data. Therefore, the credibility of your results are at stake if you delete too many cases or any cases for the wrong reason; delete only those for which you have strong reasons to believe that they threaten the reliability or validity of your study. Other strategies (which we discuss below) are often preferred. Whether you delete a case or replace a value with a marker for missing data, any rule used should be used consistently and argued, recorded, and reported thoroughly.

(a) Missing Data Missing data is a common problem that affects most data sets. In panel data or other longitudinal data, it is common to lose cases between waves of data collection as participants drop out or become unavailable. In cross-sectional organizational data, it is common for some organizations not to have certain metrics, where others do. In surveys, it is common for respondents to skip a few questions, leading to missing data for selected variables.

If few cases have missing values, these cases are typically deleted from the dataset entirely or deleted listwise (excluding a complete case from a group of related analyses) or pairwise (excluding a case only for analyses that use the missing values) during the analysis. In a multiple regression, for example, pairwise exclusion would disregard a case from the computation of parameters only for the variables where data is missing. For example, if you have a data set of 50 employees and 5 cases have missing data for age, listwise deletion would exclude these 5 employees from all analyses, while pairwise deletion would exclude them only from analyses in which age is included as an independent variable or covariate.

Despite its common use in dealing with missing data, research has shown that simply excluding cases or values introduces bias and that there are better ways to approach missing data. (For an extensive overview, see [1].) Especially when there is a large amount of missing data, we should check to see whether the missing values follow a pattern, as if they do, there is "systematicity" in the missing data. Systematicity often means that there is a good reason why the data is missing—not just that someone forgot to answer a question or that some data is not available: the empty data *means something*, so it contains or conceals important information that would influence the findings if it were excluded pairwise or listwise. In an example from our own research, we were interested in how much the bakery department in retail stores contributed to the stores' overall performance [2]. However, because smaller stores often have fewer departments, we had many missing values for the performance data of the non-bakery departments. This data was missing for a reason: the departments did not exist. In such cases, missing values have to be replaced with values computed based on the data that *is* available. In our example, we weighed the bakeries' contribution to sales by (1) calculating each type of departments' (e.g., seafood, deli, long-life) average contribution to sales across all stores, (2) multiplying this average contribution with the focal store's total sales for each of the missing departments, (3) adding the resulting estimation of the contribution of 'missing' departments to the focal store's sales, and (4) dividing the focal store's bakery sales by the weighted total sales for that store. While this weighting solution fit our specific case, there are other systematic approaches, such as least squares and maximum likelihood estimations of missing values [1]. It is worthwhile consulting at least the introductory chapter of Little and Rubin [1] to see whether your data would benefit from applying these methods.

As a general rule, ensure you report the number of cases in your original data, the number of cases excluded, and *why* they were excluded. Similarly, if you replace missing data with other values, be sure to report why and how it was done. The final sample that is left after cleaning data is often referred to as the "valid sample."

(b) Inconsistent Data (e.g., Age < Tenure) A problem similar to missing data is inconsistent data. For example, inconsistent performance data, such as when total costs exceed revenue but a profit was recorded, could indicate that the data for that case is not reliable. In surveys, instead of skipping questions, some respondents will continue completing questions without thinking about the answer, which may lead to extreme tendencies (discussed below) or improbable combinations of values. In the bakery study discussed above, a number of respondents had a value for age that was lower than the value for tenure or values for tenure in a position that were higher than values for experience in related work. These inconsistencies are indications that respondents either made a one-off mistake or lost interest in the survey, which would suggest we cannot trust the data. While one of these inconsistencies is not enough to exclude an entire case, they indicate the need for further investigation of that case. Therefore, it is always a good idea to think about the logical relationships that should hold between certain variables in your data, track cases in which this logic does not manifest, and investigate these cases' data for other inconsistencies, tendencies, or outliers. The easiest way to perform such an investigation is to create tables that combine each of the relevant categorical variables (e.g., age × tenure) and histograms of all discrete variables.

(c) Improbable Response Time In survey research, an exceptionally short response time is often a symptom of loss or lack of interest as well. However, since some people complete surveys faster than others, we should develop a credible, conservative rule for excluding cases and apply it consistently. One example is to exclude only cases with a response time that is significantly shorter than expected. (See Sect. 8.1.2(e) Outliers for information on how to define a threshold)

(d) Extreme Tendencies An extreme tendency occurs when the values for one case and multiple variables are unexpectedly high, low, or invariable. In surveys that use 7-point Likert-type response scales, this often takes the form of a series of all ones or sevens, which could reflect the respondent's loss of interest. It is often difficult to establish whether such extreme tendencies reflect an unreliable response (such as one that is due to loss of interest), a reliable response that is affected by a tendency to respond consistently, or a reliable response that is an outlier. Therefore, cases should be excluded only when tendencies are extreme, such as when more than half of the variables have the same value. With surveys it is often helpful to cross these extreme tendencies with response times, as when they indicate an unreliable response, they will often have short response times as well.

(e) Outliers Another reason to exclude cases is an extreme score, an outlier, on one or more of the variables. For example, a young, small firm with unusually high profit should be investigated further, as should a 10-year-old with a perfect score on an advanced physics exam. Outliers are cases' values for one or more variables that are so extreme that they influence the results of analyses or distort distributions (leading to violation of assumptions) because they are not valid representations of the population (e.g., a prime minister does not represent the average white collar worker) or are the result of measurement error (e.g., a 174-year-old person). The outlier cases may also be unique–a Mozart in a large classroom of music students. It is not that the Mozart data is invalid or unreliable, but it distorts the view of the general population of music students and skews what we can learn about "all others." When not marked by any of the more obvious issues, outliers are not necessarily easy to spot, especially in large data sets.

One commonly used rule is to exclude cases that are a certain distance from the mean [3], which is generally expressed in terms of the number of standard deviations, or the *z*-score is. *z*-scores, which express where a value lies relative to the other data in a sample, are calculated by (1) taking any measured value of a variable, (2) subtracting the mean score of that variable, and (3) dividing this difference by the standard deviation. In other words:

$$z = \frac{x - \bar{x}}{s}$$
$$\Rightarrow x = \bar{x} + s * z$$

The z-score is useful for a number of reasons. First, it tells us something about where a value lies relative to the mean in a variable's distribution, expressed in a number that takes the spread of the distribution into account. Taking the mean into account is important because it sets the reference point. For example, in the US, a man who is a 185 cm tall at age 20 is not exceptional, whereas the same body height is exceptional at age 14 [4]. Using the standard deviation to measure the distance from the mean is also important because the same distance from the mean can mean very different things in different populations. For example, less than 10 % of 2-year-olds are 4.5 cm taller than the average body height at their age, whereas more than 25 % of men are that much taller than average at age 20. z-scores allow us to compare scores across different data samples, which is why converting raw scores to z-scores is called standardization: we convert the data to a common standard to make it comparable.

z-scores are also useful because standardization entails forcing values into a "normal distribution," for which a number of handy rules apply. A normal distribution is a distribution for which the same number of cases can be observed to have values above and below the mean (so it is symmetric) and for which the number of observed cases per value of the variable follows a bell-shaped curve, such as that pictured in Fig. 8.1.

The normal distribution attained by replacing all of a variable's values with z-scores has a mean ($\bar{x}$) of 0, a standard deviation (s) of 1, and a predictable distribution across the range. For example, we know that 95 % of values will lie between a standard deviation of -1.96 and 1.96. For 20-year-old men in the US, these values correspond to roughly 163 cm and 190 cm. This, with a large D-tour, brings us back to outliers.

We expect that 95 % of all values lie between a z-score of -1.96 and 1.96, and about 100 % of cases lie between a z-score of -3.29 and 3.29. An observed value outside of those boundaries is highly improbable and, therefore, can be considered an outlier. The 83-year-old bowls player pictured in Fig. 8.2 shows how such an outlier *skews* the distribution of the sample. Exploring, summarizing, and visualizing data is another good way to find outliers.

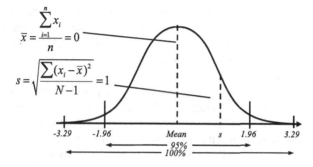

Fig. 8.1 The standard normal distribution, its mean, and its standard deviation

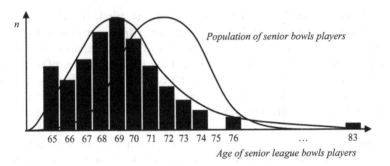

Fig. 8.2 Example of a histogram and distributions of the sample and population

8.1.3   Exploring Data: Summary Statistics and Visualization

Once your data is structured intuitively and is clean, the extraction of meaning can start. A first step in this process is exploring data by summarizing it into intuitive statistics and visualizing it. The most common intuitive summary statistics are means, medians (i.e., the middle score), and standard deviations (i.e., the average distance of values to the mean). These values are so useful in understanding the data that they are often reported as part of descriptive statistics to give readers a quick view of the sample's characteristics.

Basic descriptive statistics can be visualized in graphs like box plots, which we read about in every statistics book but do not often see used in practice. If you are interested, have a look at McGill, Tukey, and Larsen [5].

Histograms provide a bit more information about the distribution of the data in a sample. Used primarily for variables with discrete values or a limited set of intervals, histograms indicate the number of observations for each value and interval. Figure 8.2 provides an example of a histogram, with a line plotted that approximates the distribution of the data, which makes it easy to compare it to the normal distribution we would expect to see in the population. This example shows that a sample of senior league bowls players is positively skewed, as it has a relatively higher proportion of younger players.

For categorical variables it is also useful to look at cross-tabulations that give you an idea of frequencies of *combinations* of categories (e.g., men who dislike cars). For linear relationships *scatter plots* are the most insightful place to start, as they visualize data points based on an independent (x) and dependent (y) variable (Fig. 3.1). In multiple regressions, similar plots can be made for all combinations of independent and dependent variables, which can help you to spot multicollinearity (see Sect. 8.2) or potential interaction effects (Fig. 2.1). Most statistical programs allow you to add estimated lines to scatter plots (Fig. 3.2), giving you the opportunity to determine quickly whether the best fit is obtained with linear or curvilinear estimations. For example, SPSS allows you to plot an estimated line over the data and extract the explained variance (R^2) easily. If the plot and explained variance suggest that a linear estimation does not fit the data, there are other avenues to be explored, including transforming the data, testing non-linear models, and turning to non-parametric tests. Before we explore these options further, we investigate how to test our data for violations of common assumptions.

8.2 Testing Assumptions

Statistical analyses work for certain (but not all) types of data, and every statistical analysis has some assumptions about the data to which you will apply the analysis. It is not just good practice, but fundamental to ensure that your data meets the assumptions. Otherwise, the analysis will yield some numbers as results, but they will carry no meaning.

Most of the analysis methods discussed in this book are based on *parametric* tests, which make a number of assumptions about the data. If these assumptions are violated, the results of the tests cannot be trusted. Therefore, before starting to analyze your data, you must determine whether the assumptions hold or corrective action or the use of non-parametric or other tests is required.

Although different tests are based on different assumptions, many analyses make similar assumptions about "normal" data (i.e., data that occurs most often). Three assumptions are common to most of the methods discussed in this book: independence of observations, normality, and homoscedasticity (or homogeneity of variance). Regression-based models also assume that the relationship of interest is linear. We discuss each of these assumptions and provide examples of tests that can be conducted to determine whether they hold. Most statistical programs have a few standard tests they rely on, and many of the examples we use are the standard tests for SPSS, which is a relatively intuitive program for becoming familiar with data analysis. Table 8.2 summarizes some of the key assumptions you need to check for the less complex methods discussed in this book. HLM and the other methods discussed in Chap. 7 are subject to more complex sets of assumptions, but they are all combinations of the independence, normality, homogeneity, and linearity assumptions we discuss here. In fact, the assumptions generally apply to different methods in slightly different ways (e.g., homogeneity of group variance vs. variance of error terms, independence of all observations or observations at one level or within one group). Therefore, we discuss each of the assumptions generically. However, once you understand the assumptions, it will be easy to find the exact method to use in the manual or a relevant guide book for your chosen statistics tool (e.g., [6, 7]).

8.2.1 Independence of Observations

Independence of observations refers to the requirement that each observation (each value that was measured for a variable) is not influenced by other observations.

Table 8.2 Primary assumptions for selected analyses

Analysis method	Relevant assumptions
Independent group comparison (*t*, *F*, *ANOVA)*	– Independence of source and measurement – Normality of distribution of DV[a] within groups[b] – Homogeneity of variance of DV across groups
Dependent group comparisons (paired-samples *t*, repeated-measures ANOVA)	– Independence of source and measurement except between groups (i.e., within the unit of analysis) – Normality of distribution of DV within groups – Homogeneity of variance of DV group differences (i.e., sphericity; only when $k^c > 2$)
Complex group comparisons (*MANCOVA)*	– Independence of source and measurement – Multivariate normality of distribution of DVs within groups[a] – Homogeneity of covariance matrices of DVs
Regression	– Independence of error terms and sufficient independence of IVs[d] (i.e., no multicollinearitymulticollinearity) – Normality of error term distribution – Homoscedasticity of errors (i.e., homogenous at different values of the IV)
Structural equation modeling	– Multivariate normality of data – Independence of error terms

[a] Dependent variable
[b] All cases with the same value for the independent (grouping) variable(s)
[c] The number of groups
[d] Independent variable

Therefore, both the sources from which data were collected (e.g., respondents) and the measurements (e.g., scoring of survey items) must be independent. Let's talk about the source of measurement first.

Independent Sources

If we were to study board members' support for decisions, the assumption of independence of sources would require that our sample consists exclusively of board members that sit on different boards. If we have a few board members who serve on the same board, it is fair to assume that their support for decisions as recorded in the sample data is not independent, as they would be likely to have exchanged arguments related to the decision first. In experimental research, the assumption of independence requires that subjects be recruited and assigned to conditions in a random fashion. However, in social sciences research, the assumption of independence of sources is violated more often than not. It is simply too difficult to find sources of measurement that are completely independent: organizations from the same industries or geographic areas will be influenced by similar forces and influence each other more than organizations from different industries or areas, employees and systems from one organization will be influenced by similar forces and influence each other more than employees and systems from different organizations, and so forth. Even more dependence between sources is present in longitudinal research, where multiple measurements are acquired from the same source. Therefore, the assumption of independence is often factored in as "equal dependence." For example, we either compare board members who sit on the same board, or we compare board members who sit on different boards of similar organizations, or we compare board members who sit on different boards of equally dissimilar organizations, and so on. If such approaches are not possible, either multilevel models must be used to analyze the data (See Chap. 5), or the biasing effect of dependencies must be estimated and taken into account in the model testing using the techniques for dealing with endogeneity discussed in Chap. 7.

Independent Measurements
The second aspect of independence relates to the measurement itself and is often discussed under the umbrella of common source bias or common method bias. Common method bias is introduced by measuring multiple variables using the same research method, while common source bias is introduced by measuring multiple variables from the same source. Although we have discussed the independence of different sources, here we focus on the independence of measurements from the same or different sources. In social science, violations of independence are commonly caused by using cross-sectional surveys that measure independent and dependent variables from the same source using the same method and at the same point in time. As we discussed in Chap. 7, measuring independent and dependent variables at the same time means we cannot claim a causal relationship between them (because one must precede the other). Measuring independent and dependent variables from the same source and using the same method also inflates the relationship between them and between the indicators that measure the same and different constructs. Podsakoff, MacKenzie, Lee, and Podsakoff [8] provided a summary of the main problems that cause bias and Podsakoff, Scott, MacKenzie, and Podsakoff [9] studied the size of the biases. These papers provided an extensive list of biases that we recommend studying, but to summarize, common source bias and common method bias generally emerge because of:

- **respondents** who are trying to be consistent, socially desirable, and/or "nice" to each other or the researcher; who are trying to be smart about which variables are related to one another (i.e., personal theories), or who are "in a mood"
- **question wording** that suggests that one answer is better than another, that is unclear, that consistently uses the same response format (e.g., 7-point Likert-type), that entails extremely positive or negative value judgments, or that influences participants' mood
- **the order of questions**, where early questions may influence responses to later questions because of priming or suggested value judgments, survey length, and effects of the grouping of related (or unrelated) items
- the measurement of the independent and dependent variable at the **same time, place, and/or using the same instrument**.

One final issue related to dependence that is caused by how variables are measured occurs when there is too much overlap between what two variables measure, which is commonly referred to as **multicollinearity**. As Chap. 3 discusses, multicollinearity refers to the case in which more than one of the independent variables capture the same variance between cases, so they explain the same part of the variance in the dependent variable.

While these problems should be taken into account when designing research studies and surveys (see [9, 10]), they are also likely to affect data analysis. The most common effects are that variance between cases that shouldn't be related becomes related (i.e., covariance in error terms), that variables that should not be related become related, that measures for reliability and validity become inflated (or deflated, such as when grouping items of different constructs), and that the relationship between independent and dependent variables becomes inflated.

How to Test and Control for Independence

Several techniques can be used to investigate the extent of method bias and source bias and to control for them statistically. These techniques help researchers to first estimate the size of the bias by estimating relationships between variables or constructs that, theoretically, should not be there. Then these relationships are "subtracted" from the relationships in which the researcher is actually interested. Good starting points if you want more information about these methods are Chap. 7 and Podsakoff et al. [9].

How can we control for independence of observations? For group comparisons (Chap. 2), different methods need to be used when the groups of interest are dependent vs. independent (Table 2.6). Independence is primarily an issue of design when comparing groups, but for regression-based models (Chaps. 3–4) we have to check whether the error terms are unrelated and whether the independent variables are not too highly correlated before we analyze the data further.

The **error terms**, as explained in Chap. 3, are the "unsystematic" part of the variance in an observation, so that part is assumed to be unrelated to any other observations in the model. Whether error terms are related can be checked by studying residual plots [which should look like Fig. 8.4a and not like Fig. 8.5a or b], but most statistical programs also have a few standard tests that you can run. For example, SPSS has the Durbin-Watson test, which should return a value close to 2 and between 1 and 3 [3]. If error terms are related, a relationship between cases or measurements is present that is not accounted for in the model. If you can't work out theoretically what that missing relationship is, an extra "method" variable should be applied to capture that variance and extract it from the error terms (see Chap. 7).

In the case of **multicollinearity** (which is also discussed in Chap. 3), independent variables will be highly correlated (i.e., $r > 0.75$), conceptually capturing the same meaning. For example, multicollinearity is present when a dichotomous variable in a model measures *employment status* (unemployed vs. employed) and another categorical variable measures *profession* and includes a category for "unemployed." These very high correlations can usually be spotted by examining how variables are measured or inspecting the correlation matrix of all variables in your model. A frequently used statistic for multicollinearity is the Variance Inflation Factor or VIF, which should be lower than 3. There are no statistical remedies for multicollinearity, so the best approach is to find its source by inspecting the correlation matrix and the associated VIFs, and redesigning the measurements and/or model accordingly. As with any assumption, the good practice is to report the presence of multicollinearity should you violate the assumption that your model is free of it.

8.2.2 Normality

The assumption of normality, the second cornerstone of all parametric statistics, is based on the assertion that, in any sizeable population, the frequency with which the values associated with a variable are observed will follow a normal distribution (similar to the bell curve pictured in Fig. 8.1). Therefore, very low and very high values will be less frequent than values closer to the median, so the *probability* of observing extremely low or high values is small. Simplifying things dramatically (at the risk of agitating statisticians), the test statistics discussed in Chap. 2 (i.e., t and F) give us an idea of the probability of observing the difference between the means (t) or the means and variances (F) of two or more observed samples, if we assume that these samples are randomly drawn from the same population. However, these tests will provide a reliable assessment of that probability only if the population is normally distributed, the sample data represents the population accurately, and the sampling really was random (and would again return a normal distribution if repeated indefinitely). However, since our sample is our best estimate of the population and the only data we have, we test to determine whether the sample data is normally distributed and use that as a proxy for everything else. To make matters even more complex, in regression-based models (including SEM and HLM), this assumption applies to the *error terms*, not the actual data, although testing for both is done in roughly the same way.

Figure 8.3 illustrates a normal distribution and typical deviations from that normal distribution, which are defined by their *skew* and *kurtosis*. Skew refers to a "pull" toward one side, caused by a larger number of cases on one side of the mean, with the other side having a larger spread. Typically, as in Fig. 8.2, skew is caused by a few extreme values on one side of the distribution. Kurtosis is the "pointiness" of a distribution. When all cases are close to the mean, the kurtosis is positive, while negative kurtosis occurs when values are more spread out (i.e., the curve is flat rather than pointed).

An intuitive way to check for normality is to compare the data to this distribution by creating histograms or Q-Q plots. These plots compare the observed quantiles (i.e., the relative positions of values) in your data to quantiles that would be expected in perfectly normally distributed data. This means that, ideally, all points in this graph lie on the diagonal line (Fig. 8.3). If points diverge from that line, the data is not normally distributed—that is, they have skew or kurtosis. Q-Q plots can

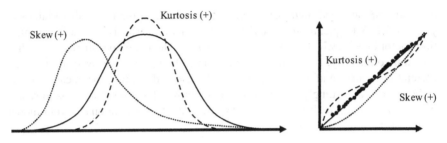

Fig. 8.3 Illustration of skew and kurtosis and how they appear in Q-Q plots

also be made for residuals in regression-based models, with the same diversions from the diagonal indicating non-normality of residuals. Most statistical programs can calculate values of skewness and kurtosis in your data or errors, and you can determine whether these are problematic by converting them into z-values (in which case they should be between -1.96 and 1.96) or by running, for example, the Shapiro-Wilks test, which returns a significant result when your data is *not* normally distributed.

8.2.3 Homogeneity of Variance and Homoscedasticity

Parametric statistical tests are based on an assessment of variable distributions, which are primarily defined by means and variances. The assumption of homoscedasticity is concerned with these variances. In group comparisons (discussed in Chaps. 2 and 6), the variance in the dependent variable should be homogenous (i.e., comparable) across the values of the independent variables (i.e., in different groups). If the variance in one group is much smaller than that in another, it would be difficult to compare the distance to the mean across both groups. Therefore, we first have to determine whether the assumption of homogeneity of variance holds. In simple group comparisons (e.g., *t*-tests or ANOVA), this check is commonly done using Levene's test or Bartlett's test for equality of variances. The null hypothesis) in both is that variances are equal, so a significant result means that they are not. If that is the case, non-parametric alternatives (e.g., Mann–Whitney or Kruskal-Wallis tests) should be used to compare the groups.

As study designs and analysis methods become more complex, the assumption of homogeneity of variance does too. The explanation we just gave applies in simple group comparisons, but in MAN(C)OVA, for example, this assumption applies to the *covariance* matrices and is commonly tested using Box's Test.

In regression-based models, the assumption takes the slightly different form of homoscedasticity, which focuses on the residuals (the distance of single points to the estimated line through the data). In this case, we are interested in the spread of residuals across the range of the independent variable(s), as homoscedasticity of residuals means that the average distance to the estimated line is the same at different values of the independent variable. In other words, if you plot the error

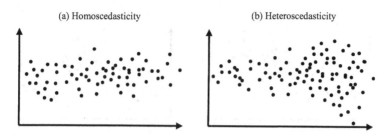

Fig. 8.4 Illustration of homoscedasticity and heteroscedasticity

terms, they should look like a reasonably "boxed" cloud. Figure 8.4 illustrates homoscedastisity and heteroscedasticity, where the cloud of dots is not boxed or reasonably straight but drops, rises, widens or narrows at some part of the line (i.e., for some values of the independent variable). Most statistical programs provide an easy option to produce plots like those in Fig. 8.4 to check your data.

Sometimes residuals will not only vary in their distance to the expected line, but also show a pattern (e.g., an increasing line or a U-shape, as illustrated in Fig. 8.5). These patterns, or "trends," suggest that there is some systematic variance in the data that is not captured by the variables in the model, and/or that the trend is not linear (which violates another assumption of regression-based models). In other words, a variable is missing from the model that explains the common variance between cases and that is related to the variables that are already part of model (as discussed extensively in Chap. 7). This relationship could be a non-linear, that is, a curvy one (e.g., quadratic). Although any of these trends may lead you to despair, they are usually a sign of interesting things happening in your data that you have not yet considered: they show that there is some systematicity in the data that you can explore and explain even though you did not expect it. Take a step back, do some more exploration, and find out where all that heterogeneous variance is coming from. Many interesting discoveries have been made by exploring initially unexplainable variance. (Think of Pavlov's dogs, for example; [11]).

8.2.4 Linearity

The last assumption we discuss in this chapter, linearity, applies to all methods that explore linear relationships between variables—surprising, isn't it. Methods like regression, structural equation modeling, and hierarchical linear modeling all explore these linear relationships, and these methods are based on the assumption that, if there is a relationship between variables in the models, it is linear—a straight line. For example, when the scatter plot of an independent (x) and dependent (y) variable looks like an inverse U-shaped cloud like shown in Fig. 8.5b, a linear estimation would tell you that the two variables are unrelated, as the best fit would be a horizontal line through the data such that β_1 is 0. However, from the graph it should be obvious that the variables have *some* relationship; it is just not a linear

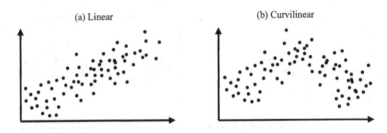

Fig. 8.5 Illustration of linear and curvilinear trends in (residual) plots

one. Similar reasoning applies to residual plots, where (as 8.5b suggests) there is a non-linear trend in the data that the model hasn't captured. The next section discusses what to do when you encounter one of these trends.

8.2.5 What if Assumptions Are Violated?

We have already discussed what to do when data is not independent, but what should you do when your data is skewed or otherwise distorted, when variances are unequal, or when relationships appear to be non-linear? The first step should always be to determine *why* the assumptions are violated. The source of the violations can often be found easily by calculating a few more descriptive statistics or visualizing your data in new ways. Once you have found the source of the problem, you can rectify your design or collect more data so you can address the problem at its source. When doing so is not possible, four popular solutions are to transform the data, to add variables to the model, to use robust and/or non-parametric tests, and to turn to non-linear methods.

Transforming the Data

Transforming the data means computing new values for new variables based on the values of the existing variables to generate a new set of data that more closely follows some of the assumptions (e.g., a normal distribution). Transformations can be linear or nonlinear. Linear transformations are the best way to go if the assumptions of normality and/or homogeneity of variances are violated but the data still resembles a normal distribution. A linear transformation subjects every value of a variable to the same manipulation (e.g., taking the logarithmic function $Log(x)$ of every value). However, care must be taken that transformations do not influence hypothesis testing or the interpretation of results. When measurements include financial data or, for example, the number of middle managers, it will be difficult or impossible to convert the effect sizes back into absolute values in order to report that "with every additional middle manager the organization loses $47.35 in annual profits." [3] provides an insightful overview of linear transformations and how to conduct them.

A common non-linear transformation is to convert a continuous variable into a categorical one. For example, when an independent variable is not normally distributed, you could use a logical cut-off point to split the cases into groups. For example, you could study students who have IQs below vs. above the population average of 100, or organizations that make a loss vs. those that make a profit. Therefore, instead of linear relationships, you will be studying groups and using the methods discussed in Chap. 2. If the dependent variable is the one to be split, logistic regression can be used (Chap. 3), or you could transform the various IQ scores into ordinal data: ordered categories such as very low (<50), reasonably low (50–75), average (75–100), and so on. However, be aware of two drawbacks of transformations into categories: First, you will lose information, as the categories ("very low," etc.) lose fine distinctions, such as the difference between an IQ score of 65 and that of 73, as in the transformed variable they would both appear as "reasonably low." Second, the composition of the ordered categories is arbitrary, as you may not agree that an IQ score of 75–100 is average.

Sometimes, for example when the assumption of linearity is violated, both linear and non-linear transformations may have to be applied in order to conduct the best possible analyses (e.g., [12]). Whichever way you transform, after applying transformations, you will need to check again to ensure that all relevant assumptions hold.

Adding Variables

Many of the violations in assumptions are caused by variance in the data that the model does not account for. These violations include variances explained by dependence between cases, the use of a common source or method, or the absence of important variables from the models. Most of these problems can be resolved by revising or extending the model so the sneaky variance that crept into other variables is correctly attributed. To learn more, refer to the discussion of endogeneity in Chap. 7 and Podsakoff et al. [9].

Using Robust and/or Non-Parametric Tests

There are alternatives for most of the parametric tests that we discuss in this book for which the assumptions discussed in this chapter are less important. Some of these tests can be used as direct non-parametric counterparts of parametric tests, such as a Spearman correlation instead of a Pearson correlation, a Mann–Whitney U instead of a t-test, or a Kruskal-Wallis test instead of an ANOVA. Discussing these options in detail would fill another book, so suffice it to state that there are many other methods. You can start an investigation of these methods by searching "robust methods for [what you want to do]." You will be amazed at the number of excellent resources available to you (e.g., [13–15]).

Non-Linear Analyses

When the assumption of linearity is violated, non-linear methods may explain more variance in the data. Simple non-linear models are very similar to regression, for example, just adding a quadratic term. If you are interested in more complex non-linear methods, we recommend Seber and Wild [16].

Now, let us see about the last remaining challenge: to *p* or not to *p*?

8.3   Mindfully Interpreting Statistics: The Case of the *p*-Value

"Good day, Amedeo. How are you today?"
"Hi, Will. I'm not too bad, although yesterday I spent all night running regressions: the beta coefficient was high and in the hypothesized direction (3.87), but the p-value was 0.058. Damn it!"
"Don't panic. Just see if you can include or add some more data."
[The next day]
"Will, I followed your advice, and now my beta coefficient is high, in the hypothesized direction (3.89), and the p-value is 0.048!"
"Ha! Awesome! I told you so! What are you doing now?"
"I'm formatting the manuscript and getting it ready for submission, of course. I owe you."

We tend to think of statistics as a process of collecting and analyzing numerical data, usually in large quantities, but statistics are also a way to represent large collections of data in summary format (e.g., the mean instead of all individual values). In this interpretation, statistics are the product, not the process. Both the process and the product of statistics are themselves fields of research in which scientists review, scrutinize, theorize, propose, counter-propose, evaluate, generate, and abandon knowledge about processes and products of statistics. Therefore, any finding about statistics and any guideline offered about the use of statistics, such as those offered in this book, are relevant only within the window of time when they were produced. Guidelines change over time.

Nothing illustrates the fallible, incomplete, and unstable nature of knowledge about statistics (or anything else, for that matter) like the current discussion about the use of the ominous *p*-value [17]. Remember that we use the *p*-value to indicate statistical significance, not the effect size or importance of the hypothesized theoretical relationship. You may have noticed in the preceding chapters that *p*-values appear often. Many scholars naturally associate statistics with *p*-values: "you are doing quantitative analysis? What is your *p*-value?"

In this section, we want to discuss the problems with this emphasis on the *p*-value. In quantitative research, in the social sciences and elsewhere, the thresholds commonly associated with *p*-values (typically 0.05, 0.01 or 0.001) are laden with significance, to the point that entire careers can hinge on some data analysis showing whether you "made" a particular level or not [18]. For many, especially young scholars, the value of 0.05 is often the breakpoint between truth and irrelevancy, between publishable result and the circular file, between failed and successful study between a promotion or a failed application. As Bettis et al. [18] put it, "Particular *p*-values (0.05, 0.01 or 0.001) have been endowed with almost mythical properties." The obsession with *p*-value has also led to some bad practices [19], such as HARKing (Hypothesizing After Results are Known) and *p*-Hacking (manipulating, transforming, testing, and analyzing data until some statistically significant result emerges). The so-called chrysalis effect [20] occurs when awful results at the beginning become awesome as research and data analysis unfold.

There are several issues at hand here. The first is the all too common misinterpretation of what the *p*-value means. Most believe a *p*-value below a certain commonly accepted threshold (e.g., < 0.05) implies that you can safely reject the null hypothesis of no effect because the *probability that the null hypothesis is correct is p* (e.g., smaller than 5 %). This interpretation is simply wrong.

Imagine you just analyzed your data and found that $p < 0.05$ for some statistical test you have done. Does this mean any of the following statements is true [21]?

1. You have disproved the null hypothesis (i.e., there is no difference between the groups in the underlying population).
2. You have found the probability that the null hypothesis is true (i.e., there is a smaller than 5 % chance that there is no difference between groups in the underlying population).
3. You have proved the experimental hypothesis (i.e., there is a difference between the treatment and control groups).
4. You can deduce the probability that the experimental hypothesis is true (i.e., there is a less than 5 % probability that there is a difference between population means).
5. If you reject the null hypothesis, you know the probability (< 0.05) that you are wrong.
6. You have a reliable experimental finding in the sense that if, hypothetically, the experiment were repeated many times, you would obtain a significant result 95 % of the time.

As a matter of fact, all six statements are incorrect. The first issue is that *p*-values make statements about samples, not populations. The *p*-value *does not express* the conditional probability that the null hypothesis) is true given the sample value, or prob(H_0 is true | sample). It expresses the opposite conditional probability prob (sample | H_0 is true), so the obtained sample value is at least as large (or small, depending) as would be observed in the sample if the null hypotheses were true! For example, based on a significant ANOVA, we could (erroneously) state that "given the magnitude of the difference between the two samples we observed, the probability that they were drawn from one and the same population is smaller than 0.05," rather than (correctly) stating that "if both samples were drawn from the same population and all other assumptions hold, the probability of observing a difference between the two samples that is at least this large is 0.05." This distinction is fundamental because we cannot simply reverse conditional probabilities [22]: while the probability that someone will die if he or she is hanged is large, the opposite— the probability that someone will be hanged if he or she is dead—is small!

The second key issue is that all statistics are misleading or incomplete when they are seen in isolation. This holds for the *p*-value just as much as for any other known statistic. The average of a population isn't very interesting or meaningful as a statement about a population, which is why we usually consider the average together with other statistics, such as the standard deviation (the average distance from the mean). As discussed in Chap. 2, a large difference between the mean scores of two groups is much more meaningful if the standard deviation for both groups is small.

The case of the *p*-value is similar: The *p*-value itself does not say much about a finding or outcome of a statistical test because *p*-values can be manipulated (e.g., by increasing the sample size or reversing hypotheses) and because a *p*-value expresses only a probability of attributing a result to chance or randomness, not the magnitude or importance of the observation itself. Unfortunately, it has become common practice to rely only on the *p*-value to argue the relevance or importance of a particular finding from data analysis.

The third issue is that the thresholds or cut-off values for what is a good or bad *p*-value result are arbitrary. Simply put, $p < 0.05$ is a *conventional threshold* that someone suggested some time ago. There is little theoretical or statistical reason that the thresholds shouldn't be 0.08, 0.0374, or any other value.

The good news is that these old views, and these three key issues, are being challenged, literally as we write this book (in 2015 and 2016). In fact, while we were writing these chapters, new guidelines, have slowly been forthcoming (e.g., [17]). While these guidelines, too, will be challenged, refined and evaluated, at this time we can make one simple, general recommendation for scholars engaging in quantitative analysis: **Always use, interpret, and report *p*-values in context**. While statisticians continue to work on whether to keep the *p*-value and with what to replace it, it appears that the most prudent possible way to deal with *p*-values is to follow these guidelines:

1. **Do not base scientific conclusions only on whether a *p*-value passes a specific threshold**: Do not argue that some result is better or worse only because some test is under or over a *p*-value threshold (such as 0.05). Always report the exact *p*-values (e.g., $p = 0.049$ or $p = 0.051$), as opposed to $p < 0.01$, 0.05 or some other threshold. Do not use a conventional 5 % level.
2. **Proper inference requires full reporting and transparency**: Always report the *p*-value together with the standard error and the confidence interval (lower and upper limit) of the estimation or test statistic. For example, if you compare two means, include the confidence interval of the test statistic (e.g., the mean difference). For coefficients, confidence intervals allow readers to evaluate the distance from 0 or 1. A useful source for calculating confidence intervals is [23].
3. **Do not use statistical significance to measure the size of an effect or the importance of a result**: Always report and discuss the effect size of an estimation together with *p*-values. In an example from medicine, meta-analyses have shown that antibiotics reduce the average duration of acute bronchitis (eight to nine days) by half a day [24], which is a statistically significant, yet irrelevant difference.
4. **Always review your interpretation of the statistics in the text** of the paper or thesis, making sure that you interpret the values appropriately and carefully. In

particular, do not use terminology such as "accepting" or "rejecting" hypotheses, and try to calculate back the effect sizes to real differences in the variables (e.g., "a difference of 27 IQ points").

At this point, you may have noticed that we ourselves do not closely follow these suggestions in this book. In other words, we are also guilty of some of the bad habits we discuss here. To some extent, this is normal; as science, knowledge, and statistics evolve, so does our learning. Some of the articles, recommendations, and statements on which we have based our discussion [17–19] have been published (or accepted for publication) while we were writing this book. Many of the examples we use (including calculation and reporting of statistics) were performed and published long before these guidelines were available, and to some extent even before researchers from our fields became aware of the discussion. Also, we needed to make sure that we soundly introduced and explained the key concepts and procedures of the different analyses. Clearly, debating some of the key metrics at that time would not have been a very good pedagogical strategy. However, at this point in the book, it is important to reinforce a key lesson: do not repeat mistakes, and do not stick to habits just because they once were or remain acceptable when you already know they are bad habits. For example, here and now we advise you to always calculate, report and interpret confidence intervals—even though we have omitted them from many of our examples in previous chapters.

With that, we have said about all we want to say about data, assumptions, and p-values. A popular saying has it that "assumptions are the mother of all . . ." well, problems. This statement is especially true when it comes to analyzing quantitative data. If the relevant assumptions for the analysis method you use do not hold, the results and conclusions drawn cannot be trusted, so you should check and correct or change course.

Much in the same vein, the last word about p-values has not yet been written. Keep track of developments communicated by influential sources for science (e.g., [25, 26]) and the top journals in your field. We certainly will.

References

1. Little RJA, Rubin DB (2014) Statistical analysis with missing data, 2nd edn. Wiley, New York
2. Mertens W, Recker J, Kummer T-F, Kohlborn T, Viaene S (2016) Constructive deviance as a driver for performance in retail. J Retail Consum Serv 30:193–203
3. Field AP (2013) Discovering statistics using IBM SPSS statistics, and sex and drugs and rock 'n' roll, 4th edn. Sage, London
4. Centers for Disease Control and Prevention, National Center for Health Statistics (2009) http://www.cdc.gov/growthcharts/clinical_charts.htm#Set1. Retrieved Mar 2016
5. McGill R, Tukey JW, Larsen WA (1978) Variations of Box plots. Am Stat 32(1):12–16, 10.2307/2683468
6. Crawley MJ (2013) The R book, 2nd edn. Wiley, West Sussex
7. Stevens JP (2009) Applied multivariate statistics for the social sciences. Taylor and Francis, London

8. Podsakoff PM, MacKenzie SB, Lee J-Y, Podsakoff NP (2003) Common method bias in behavioral research: a critical review of the literature and recommended remedies. J Appl Psychol 88(5):879–903

9. Podsakoff PM, MacKenzie SB, Podsakoff NP (2012) Sources of method bias in social science research and recommendations on how to control it. Annu Rev Psychol 63(1):539–69. doi:10.1146/annurev-psych-120710-100452

10. Conway JM, Lance CE (2010) What reviewers should expect from authors regarding common method bias in organizational research. J Bus Psychol 25(3):325–34. doi:10.1007/s10869-010-9181-6

11. Fredholm L (2001) Ivan Petrovich Pavlov (1849–1936). http://www.nobelprize.org/educational/medicine/pavlov/readmore.html. Retrieved Mar 2016

12. Cheung CMK, Lee MKO (2009) User satisfaction with an internet-based portal: an asymmetric and nonlinear approach. J Am Soc Inf Sci Technol 60(1):111–122

13. Andersen R (2008) Modern methods for robust regression. Sage, Los Angeles

14. Hox J, van de Schoot R (2013) Robust methods for multilevel analysis. In: Scott MA, Simonoff JS, Marx BD (eds) The SAGE handbook of multilevel modeling. Sage, Thousand Oaks, CA, pp 387–402

15. Wilcox RR (2012) Introduction to robust estimation and hypothesis testing, 3rd edn. Academic, New York

16. Seber GAF, Wild CJ (2003) Nonlinear regression. Wiley, Hoboken, NJ

17. Wasserstein RL, Lazar NA (2016) The ASA's statement on P-values: context, process, and purpose. Am Stat. doi:10.1080/00031305.2016.1154108

18. Bettis RA, Ethiraj S, Gambardella A, Helfat C, Mitchell W (2016) Creating repeatable cumulative knowledge in strategic management. Strategic Manage J 37(2):257–261

19. Starbuck WH (2016) 60th Anniversary Essay: How journals could improve research practices in social science. Admin Sci Q. doi:10.1177/0001839216629644

20. O'Boyle EH Jr, Banks GC, Gonzalez-Mulé E (2016) The chrysalis effect: how ugly initial results metamorphosize into beautiful articles. J Manage (in press)

21. Gigerenzer G (2004) Mindless statistics. J Socio-Econ 33(5):587–606

22. Branch M (2014) Malignant side effects of null-hypothesis significance testing. Theory Psychol 24(2):256–277

23. Altman D, Machin D, Bryant T, Gardner M (2013) Statistics with confidence: confidence intervals and statistical guidelines. Wiley, New York

24. Smith SM, Fahey T, Smucny J, Becker LA (2014) Antibiotics for acute bronchitis. Cochrane Database of Systematic Reviews (3) Art No: CD000245. doi:10.1002/14651858.CD000245.pub3. www.cochranelibrary.com

25. Baker M (2016) Statisticians issue warning over misuse of P values: policy statement aims to halt missteps in the quest for certainty. Nature 531:151. doi:10.1038/nature.2016.19503

26. Nuzzo R (2014) Scientific method: Statistical errors—P values, the 'gold standard' of statistical validity, are not as reliable as many scientists assume. Nature 506(7487):150–152. doi:10.1038/506150a

Keeping Track and Staying Sane

Here this books draws to a close, but your efforts in data analysis continue. As we are sure you know, conducting data analyses can be long, tedious, and confusing. Some of us enjoy digging around, trying new things, and looking at new software and new ways of collecting, treating, and analyzing data, and we get excited about results and what they might mean. On the other hand, the absence of good data, good findings, clear outcomes, and a clear understanding of what they mean can weigh heavily. Even so, rest assured that there are some tricks to get you going and keep you going.

First, so you don't lose too much time, your temper, or your mind, keep track of what you are doing. Keeping track begins before you start analyzing and, ideally, even before you start collecting data, and doing so is vital when you are doing the analysis. Try keeping a log book. Which tests did you run? Which variables did you use? Which transformations have you tried? This kind of record is useful not only for yourself but also for journal editors and the scientific community, both of which are increasingly scrutinizing the research process, not just the results.[1]

Second, when designing your study, try to think about the design for your data analyses as well. Plan how you will structure your data, clean it, test assumptions, and analyze it to obtain answers to your research questions. Thinking about these issues before you gather data will ensure that you don't overlook an important variable or that you measure variables at the wrong level or in an unsuitable format. An excellent source that will help you plan your study design is Chap. 5 in Recker (2012).[2] The key is to ask yourself during research design what the data you generate will look like and whether it will be the data you need to answer your questions.

---

[1]Check out this amazing service offered for free to the scientific community: http://retractionwatch.com/

[2]Recker, Jan (2012) Scientific Research in Information Systems: A Beginner's Guide. Heidelberg, Germany: Springer.

© Springer International Publishing Switzerland 2017
W. Mertens et al., *Quantitative Data Analysis*, DOI 10.1007/978-3-319-42700-3_9

Third, go beyond the interface. Some statistical software packages allow you to click your way through analyses, but most (like STATA, SAS, and Matlab) also allow you to write the program or structure of commands (also called syntax) for the analysis. Even the "what you see is what you get" programs allow you to see, store, and edit the syntax behind every analysis—for example, just click "paste" instead of "ok" in SPSS—and run analyses using syntax only. (Open a new one by clicking file → new → syntax). It is helpful to look at the syntax, save it, and understand it, as doing so gives you control over what you are trying to do. Therefore, once you start analyzing, it is a good idea to store the syntax for each of the analysis steps, including (notes about) the results, why you ran that analysis, whether it returned the desired results and why (not), and on which assumptions you based the analysis. Doing so will allow you to go back at any point to see why you made a certain analysis choice or how you obtained your reported results. Here is an example from a "cleaning" phase that was written in SPSS syntax. Note how the software instructions (the capitalized statements) are interspersed with commentary (the italicized statements that begin with an asterisk) to guide future readers of the instructions about what is happening:

Replaced all dates in the variable 'time' (time of starting survey) with the same date in the style of the 'SubmitDate' variable, e.g. 2014-05-06 with 6-May-2014; then computed the completion time by calculating time between both; then excluded bottom outliers only (they were allowed to abandon and complete survey later).

using "Compute Date and Time Wizard" : compute Start_time.
COMPUTE Start_time=number(Time, DATETIME20).
VARIABLE LABELS Start_time 'Start Time'.
VARIABLE LEVEL Start_time (SCALE).
FORMATS Start_time (DATETIME20).
VARIABLE WIDTH Start_time(20).
EXECUTE.

using "Date and Time Wizard" : calculate Completion_time.
COMPUTE Completion_time = DATEDIF(SubmitDate, Start_time, "minutes").
VARIABLE LABELS Completion_time "Completion time in minutes".
VARIABLE LEVEL Completion_time (SCALE).
FORMATS Completion_time (F5.0).
VARIABLE WIDTH Completion_time(5).
EXECUTE.

Exclude outliers based on completion time (pc 5 = 10 min; computed based on Z-score)
DATASET ACTIVATE DataSet1.
FILTER OFF.
USE ALL.
SELECT IF (Completion_time >= 10).
EXECUTE.
Note: AGGREGATE can be used to compute mean scores per store (break variable: store)
to MATCH performance with survey data: first sort based on store_nr, then MATCH:

Also keep track of the number of cases with which you began; how many you excluded and why; how you recombined, transformed, or recoded variables (including any labels you assigned); which variables you corrected because of violations of assumptions and how; and how many times you opened the fridge or went for another cup of coffee you didn't finish. Because, you know, why not?

Fourth, apart from tracking what you do, writing it down, and planning, find a buddy who is also analyzing data who can perform "common-sense checks" for you—and you for him or her. Even if the methods you are using to analyze your data differ, and whether you are using the same or different data, it is important to have the opportunity to explain to someone else how you are analyzing your data and why. Explaining will help you double-check your own assumptions and plan, and while it can be difficult to spot faults in your own reasoning, it is often easy to spot them in other peoples' analyses. An added benefit is that you will learn a little about your buddy's methods. In fact, that is how this book started: by sharing insights about new analysis methods with colleagues we met over coffee. Informal chats turned into a seminar we held together, the seminar turned into a workshop series, the series turned into a book, and here we are.

Just remember the adage from, perhaps, A.E. Houseman,[3] especially if the data just won't do what you want it to do—"Statistics are used too much like a drunk uses a lamppost: for support, not illumination"—and do not act like a drunk!

---

[3]http://www.brainyquote.com/quotes/quotes/v/vinscully205138.html?src=t_statistics;   http://quoteinvestigator.com/2014/01/15/stats-drunk/

Index

A
Additivity, 24
Aggregation, 64–67
  inter-rater agreement, 66
Agreement, 24, 38, 65–67
Alpha, 3, 10, 103
Analysis of variance (ANOVA)
  multivariate analysis of covariance
    (MANCOVA), 15, 16, 26
  multivariate ANOVA, 14–15
  one-way ANOVA, 10–13
Assumptions, 2, 9, 10, 12, 15, 16, 24, 28, 31,
    34, 41, 46, 47, 54, 57, 62, 63, 68, 71,
    79, 82, 88, 91, 93, 136–155,
    157–159
Attrition, 75
Average variance extracted (AVE), 50

B
Beta coefficient, 22, 32, 152
Box plots, 142
Breusch-Pagan Lagrange multiplier test, 92

C
Causality, 11, 17, 55, 81, 103
Chi square (χ^2), 48
Clustering
  one-way, 80, 81
  time-series, 79
  two-way, 81
Coefficient of determination, 23, 29, 31–33, 35,
    36, 48, 90, 91, 109, 111, 143. *See
    also* R squared (R^2)
Constant, 2, 28, 33, 40, 104
Construct
  formative, 55, 56
  latent, 40, 46, 50

reflective, 54, 55
Correlation (r)
  cross-sectional, 77, 79, 80
  time-series/serial, 77, 79, 80
Covariance, 16
Cronbach's alpha, 50, 56, 66, 67
Cross-sectional dependency, 77, 79, 81

D
Data
  longitudinal, 63, 70, 74–75, 77, 79, 81–85,
    96, 138
  missing, 138–139
  multilevel, 34, 136
  nested, 3, 61–71, 136
  panel
    balanced, 74
    unbalanced, 74
Descriptive statistics, 8, 10, 26–28, 31, 32, 109,
    115, 129, 142, 150

E
Effect size, 3, 12, 13, 28, 63, 150, 152, 154, 155
Endogeneity, 17, 81, 88, 97, 103
Endogenous predictor, 112, 120
Error term (ε_i)
  error distribution, 24
  error variance, 54, 63
Eta squared (η^2), 12
  partial, 14, 15
Exclusion restrictions, 114, 118–121, 123, 124,
    126
Exogeneity, 122
Experiment
  between-subjects experimental design, 75
  natural, 114, 120
  randomized, 103, 104

© Springer International Publishing Switzerland 2017
W. Mertens et al., *Quantitative Data Analysis*, DOI 10.1007/978-3-319-42700-3

Printed in the United States
By Bookmasters